DIALED - IN
Jan Opperman's Story

JOHN SAWYER

This Edition Published by:

A Division of Veloce Enterprises Inc.
7800 IH 10 West, Suite 100
San Antonio, TX 78230

Softbound Edition, September 2006

ISBN: 1-58850-063-2

For a complete list of books and manuals available from VelocePress please visit our website:

www.VelocePress.com

Originally Published by:

Carl Hungness Publishing
P. O. Box 24308
Speedway, IN 46224

First Printing: May, 1981

ISBN: 0-915088-28-2

Library of Congress Catalog Card No.: 81-82108

"I'm a spirit-filled man, who wants to share what he has received from his Lord. I love you all and look forward to seein' you all at the Victory banquet. 'Tis for sure amazing grace that all us folks are part of that mighty victory."

Your brother,

Jan

Table of Contents

Introduction

Some people, not well-versed in auto racing jargon, may be confused by the title of this book. "Dialed-In" is, for sure, a racer's expression . . . meaning that a driver and a particular car are tuned in to each other and, as a team, they are likewise tuned in to a particular track that is about to be challenged. In short, "Dialed-In" — as a figure of speech — indicates the right setup is present for winning.

Choosing a title for a volume devoted to Jan Opperman's life was never a problem. The above-explained, "left turn only" lingo just had to be it. For one thing, "Opp" was the first of his breed to use the expression in my presence. This isn't to say that he was the inventor of the catchy term, just that he was responsible for introducing it to my vocabulary.

Secondly, there is the matter of Opperman's racing record — especially in Sprint Cars. For those who have seen him do his thing in the "side-bite" machines, few could have doubted that Jan has generally been well "Dialed-In". A check with some of those who have chased him around a hundred dust-choked tracks could probably further establish the fact.

But there is more to my title choice than is represented by skillful broadsliding, clever gear selection or the proper grooving of Firestone Drag Tires. Through acceptance of Christ and because of his basic compassionate nature, "Opp" has truly put his house in order. He loves his fellow man (especially those who are hurting); in or out of a race car, he stands on solid ground; and most importantly — Beaver Crossing, Nebraska's most famous resident is really "Dialed-In" with life.

So much has been written about Jan Opperman; few race drivers have commanded more publicity. He has been labeled, relabeled and then labeled again. "Self-proclaimed hippie", "dirt track champion", "Jesus Freak", "shootin'-up needle freak" . . . on and on the journalistic categorizing has made its merry way. A few members of the typewriter clan have even sought vivid descriptions of his physical person . . . long hair of the consistency of steel wool, eyes that resemble those of a high-country timber wolf and so forth. As Jan would say, "Whew, that's heavy stuff."

Much of the printed material has been factual, or at least reasonably so. If this country has produced a legitimate dirt track champion in the last twenty years, then the honor must go to Opperman. Likewise, Jan was a hippie . . . as much as anyone could be. Most likely he still is, even though the species has supposedly become extinct. I say that because even forty thousand dollar yearly earnings never really changed his lifestyle . . . the same old Ford Station Wagon and faded Levis prevailed.

But a "shootin'-up needle freak" — not Jan Opperman. He was never into that kind of thing, and don't ever call him a "Jesus Freak", either. As for timber wolf eyes . . . not being an expert on ocular variations, I shall leave that observation for those more qualified to evaluate. His eyes are unusual — no doubt about that. They seem to radiate a well-defined sincerity, a certain inner tranquility. Maybe that's why it's tough to talk with Jan and fail to look him right in the eye.

The following chapters present Jan Opperman's story. Tough, California street brawler; peace and love advocate; Twentieth Century Disciple of Christ; dirt-slinging, fence-crunching Sprint Car racer and miracle worker at Indy . . . it is all here. Through my hand, "Opp" explains both where he has been and where he hopes to go.

In a sense it is my story also. Lost and drifting through life — wondering who I was and why — my aimless path fortunately intersected the more positive trail of Jan Opperman. That was long ago but I well remember his message and other messages that have followed.

> "Stop laying all those negative thoughts on yourself. Recognize who you are and accept it. And brother — give The Man (God) a chance — admit that you can't control everything. Put a little love in your heart and take things as they come. You will be surprised how much more beauty there is to see."

Today I am a stronger man because of "Oppie". I like to think I have more compassion, more tolerance and an improved self image. Let us just say that this old outlaw is a little better "Dialed-In".

Ironically, I was later to share one of Jan's darkest hours. In 1976 when a Champ-Dirt Car dumped him on his head and another of the high-winding beasts slammed into him at full throttle, this writer was one of the first to reach the scene. I helped drag his apparently-lifeless body from the wreckage . . . out through the smoke and steam to safety. As did many others, waiting for the ambulance, I knelt beside him on the blood-stained soil to pray.

"Not to knock the doctors, but I believe those prayers saved me," Jan later said. "Even the medicos had me a D.O.A. statistic."

From my corner, I hope Jan is correct. There was little for any of us to do but pray and a world without "Opp" would have been a bleak one, at best.

In conclusion, when my first book (The Dusty Heroes) was completed, I swore there would never be another. Too much hassle, too much time, too much of everything . . . but then I thought about Jan Opperman. There just had to be a book about his amazing life and, as his friend, I should be the man to write it. So, here we go again . . . it is simply my way of saying thanks.

In The Shadow Of Death

The long, bronze-colored race car pounded a path through the myriad of rubber-glazed ruts in a defiant quest for dirt track immortality. Its driver — clad in a blue, flame-retardant uniform and purple helmet (accented by a cross) — pumped the steering wheel with computerized, mechanical violence. From lock position to lock position, his powerful arms wrestled the twisting wheel in an urgent effort to prevent the machine's right rear tire from breaking traction on the slippery clay.

Like an enraged animal, the car's Chevrolet engine howled and roared over nearly every inch of the eight furlongs of earth, commonly referred to by racers as "The Big Mile". For a moment, just prior to the approach of each corner, the steaming motor would be backed off. Equally as fast, the driver's foot pressed the throttle to send more of the volatile methanol into each of the eight cylinders and the relentless, deafening struggle resumed.

Well that it might have been, for both the bronze car and its brightly dressed chauffeur were challenging for the lead in America's richest and most prestigious dirt racing event — run with open-cockpit cars. Labeled The Hoosier Hundred, this classic extravaganza in automotive nostalgia has been held with ritualistic regularity these last twenty-five years at the Indiana State Fairgrounds (Indianapolis) . . . usually in

September. September 11, 1976 being the date for the particular race in discussion. Sanctioned by the United States Auto Club, the action is provided by a field of twenty-four Championship Dirt Cars.*

During the above-mentioned quarter century, all the great names in "topless" speed competition have driven The Hoosier Hundred and some of them have been fortunate enough to emerge victorious . . . A. J. Foyt, Jim Bryan, Jud Larson, Al Unser, Parnelli Jones and Mario Andretti — to name a few. One hundred laps over one mile of trembling, pitted turf — only the fiercest of an already fierce legion would ever know the exultation of triumph in such a test.

Now Jan Opperman (the man in blue with the cross on his helmet) was trying to join that exclusive membership. Opperman, a veritable legend on the clay, had won a ton of dirt track races in his time, but this had the makings of his biggest win. For fifty laps he had ridden in the exact shadow of the front-running car of Johnny Parsons, Jr.; just a blink of an eye separating the rampaging machines.

Like prima ballerinas in some grandiose, mechanized ballet, the two rocketing objects slid through the turns — welded together in their deadly dance. Left front wheels lifted off the ground in unison, helmeted heads snapped back and forth in perfect cadence and great streamers of moist earth exploded off the outside rear tires of each car. With a splat, the sticky clay cascaded against the outer retaining wall. The very ribbon of concrete that lurked only inches from the clutching, tearing treads of Goodyear's finest.

On lap fifty-one, the two leaders came by my vantage point — inside turns three and four — virtually side by side. Front wheels cranked hard right against the slides, right-side shocks

*Championship Dirt Cars are the anachronistic darlings of American motorsport. Engines up front; long, graceful tail sections, artistically enameled with enormous numbers . . . these awesome vehicles are throwbacks to another era. A long ago time when mile-length dirt ovals were the traditional theaters of open-cockpit racing with gilded legends like Ted Horn and Rex Mays playing the leading roles. Sadly, in today's racing, the great cars are put on display only four or five times a year at selected sites like the Indiana Fairgrounds.

bottomed completely out . . . the straining engines thundering along in a fuel-injected harmony. Through the blur of dirt-smeared goggles, Opperman studied his solitary opponent intently. It wasn't hard to imagine the thought process ricocheting about within the confines of that stone-chipped helmet.

> "John, I am determined to win this race," Jan had told me earlier, after time trials. "We've had some rough luck with our car this year, but we're hooked-up today . . . really dialed-in. If I can't get the lead early, I'll bide my time. No wild chances 'cause — Praise God — I know it's our day."

A flutter in the rpm level of the bronze car's motor indicated that a decision had been made. Jan Opperman had backed off the gas — just a bit. For now he was content to remain the stalker and a fateful decision that would prove to be. In a flash, the brace of hard-sliding pace setters skillfully unwrapped themselves from turn four and shot into the comparative sanity of the main straightaway. Down that undeviating route they dashed — nose to tail — headed for the fifty-second lap and a rendezvous with disaster.

Close behind — reaching into an apparent, dusty infinity — came the frantic followers led by Bubby Jones, their engines snapping, cracking and belching flames from red-hot header pipes. With psychedelic inconsistency, the 100 mile an hour collage of brilliant colors darted in and out of the tawny mist that spread its eerie glow over everything. Dazed by the brutal pace, drivers reflexively turned their heads against the barrage of earthen shrapnel that attacked men and machine with equal cruelty.

Then, within my field of vision, it was again the battle for first place. High and fast they drifted through the third corner's sweeping expanse. For an instant all seemed to be in order — the same two cars, the same two drivers.

But dirt track auto racing pays little heed to order and it has no regard for sameness. Things happen, changes come about and so do the violent crashes . . . fast — faster even than the best reflexes available to mortals.

Parsons' race-leading machine broke traction in its hurried exit from the slippery turn three. With an amazing lack of grace, the car's lengthy tail section whipped around creating a half-spin that headed it straight for the outside wall. Afforded only a fraction of a second to react, Opperman ripped his steering wheel hard left to dive under the slowing vehicle — a scant few feet in front of him.

He almost made it . . . so close but yet so far. His right front wheel, probing desperately for a clear path, struck the front end of the other car. Up and over he went . . . a quick end for end flip and then a slow roll to land upside down, directly in the middle of the speedy rim-riders' groove. Crash — Bubby Jones piled headlong into the disabled twosome, but the worst was yet to come.

Confusion reigned supreme as the remainder of the field sought to avoid the carnage that blocked a good portion of the race track. For a moment it appeared to be a merciful possibility. One by one and in groups, the unbelievable skills of these drivers allowed them to, somehow, slither through the narrow openings available for escape.

A. J. Foyt got through and so did Joe Saldana — however, it was too much to expect. Two unfortunate cars were pinned against the outside wall in this full-throttle evasive action. There being absolutely no room to maneuver, the inevitable happened.

Blinded by billowing dust and understandably bewildered by the chaotic display ahead of him, one young driver — Chuck Gurney from Livermore, California — found himself headed right for the overturned bronze car and its stunned rider, trapped inside. With a thunderous bang, Gurney's 1500 pound missile slammed savagely into the cockpit section where Opperman was hanging, head down, in his safety harness. Pieces of sheet metal and chunks of fiber glass leaped into the air. The entire area seemed to vibrate with the violence of the impact.

Then there was the silence. For a moment nothing moved, not a sound could be heard. That awful stillness, so often following a tragedy and fairly reeking of death, was everywhere. A lonesome, hollow thing that paralyzes your very will to live.

The first to react was Chuck Gurney, who by some stroke of good fortune had emerged from the shattering collision unscathed. Grief-stricken by the horrible circumstances that had involved his presence in such a debacle, he wriggled free from the destruction of his own car and rushed to the aid of Jan Opperman.

"Oh my God, oh my God," he screamed in utter anguish. "Please help me get him out of here . . . PLEASE!!! Oh God, he's hurt so bad."

In a matter of seconds, with reinforcements on the scene, Jan's motionless figure was dragged free of the fuel-soaked wreckage. "He can't breathe in that stuff — get that helmet and dirt mask off," someone shouted. Very gingerly, both items were removed, to be followed by the blood-soaked nomex hood. Only then did each of us fully realize that one of our best friends was possibly gone forever.

"Oppie's" face was expressionless — covered with the vagueness of lost life. His eyes . . . wide open and empty, staring at nothing, were glazed over. There was no sign of breathing, no flaring at his nostrils and a grayish dust seemed to be settling over him.

"Wake up, Jan, come on, Jan . . . you're gonna be O.K. . . . nobody can kill you," begged Bubby Jones, kneeling beside his long-time friend. Apparently convinced that no reply was possible, he straightened up and turned in my direction. Angrily he blinked at the tears which were etching tiny, muddy trails across his face. "Why did it have to be him?" he asked. "Damn, of all people, not 'Opp' — he's better'n all of us." With that final remark he slammed down the visor on his Bell Star Helmet, as if to shut out the horror of the moment.

By then the emergency team had arrived and Jan

Opperman was loaded inside the ambulance. A young doctor whispered some awesome words, as the back door was closed. "If you know his wife, you better help her, 'cause I don't think he's gonna make it," he said to me.

"You'll probably see her before I can, she's got pneumonia and is already in the hospital," I replied, my voice choked to a hiss.

"Oh wow," the doctor gasped . . . and then he jumped into the ambulance as it pulled away. Amidst the wailing of sirens and flashing of lights, the most important race of Jan Opperman's life was underway.

All alone in the middle of the track — his scarlet driving uniform soaked with sweat — stood Chuck Gurney. His shoulders heaved convulsively as he sobbed — quite near the point of hysteria.

I remember putting my arm around him in an attempt to ease his pain, but there was no consoling Gurney.

"An accident, you say," his words came to me garbled by grief. "It wasn't my fault, you say . . . what's the matter with us? We just drive these damned things and look what happens." Pausing to catch his breath between sobs, he continued. "If Jan dies, if Jan dies . . . I'll never . . . thanks, but I just wanta be alone."

Watching Chuck Gurney trudge off and daubing at my own eyes, I decided that there had been more than one casualty of the 1976 Hoosier Hundred.

Say A Prayer For Jan

"Thanks very much for the award . . . it's an honor. But there's somethin' else that should be done at this time. We should say a prayer for Jan Opperman, 'cause he really needs it. Jan has prayed for all of us and now he really needs some help."

The hushed voice, issuing those words over the track loudspeaker system, was that of Bubby Jones. Up on the judge's stage, at the Hoosier's conclusion, Jones had just been recognized as the event's 1976 Rookie-of-the-Year. Obviously his thoughts lay considerable distance from any personal achievement . . . most likely deep within the innards of Indianapolis Methodist Hospital, where Opperman's life had either become history or he was still fighting for it.

Actually, the prayers for Jan had begun an hour or so earlier — before his critically-injured body had been placed aboard the ambulance. Queenie Leavell (wife of driver Rich Leavell, both of whom were close friends of the Oppermans), Johnny Coogan (a driver and mechanic) and some others had organized a concerted effort to bring about "Opp's" salvation — one way or the other. The consensus being that neither tears nor any amount of wailing would do Jan any good. It was up to the Lord and somebody had better start getting a message through to him.

Yet this takes nothing away from Jones' dramatic announcement. Those words remain among my most treasured auto racing memories and I can hear them plainly to this day. Likewise, I can still see his gaunt figure standing on that dirt-flecked stage . . . longish hair blowing in the breeze, the pale, moisture-laden eyes, and a soft voice magnified barely above a whisper.

Later on, upon arriving at Methodist Hospital, many members of the racing fraternity (myself included) received a graphic illustration of a significant portion of Jan's philosophy, which he had often shared with us. Namely, the power of positive prayer as opposed to negativism. A number of people, again myself included, had been too negative. Jan Opperman was alive — barely so — but he was alive.

As soon as possible, he was moved from the Emergency Room area to the hospital's Intensive Care section, where his critical condition could be handled by the variety of life-support systems available. The array of folks that gathered in the somber waiting room was amazing in its scope. Bobby Hillin, Jan's car owner; Donnie Ray Everett, his chief mechanic, and their associates, sat in a hushed conversation in one corner. Steve Shultz (badly injured himself, in an early-season accident) visited quietly with driver and race-tire merchant, Duke Cook. "Lil" Joe Saldana, the winner of the ill-fated race, stood alone — his face ashen, his dark eyes glued to the doorway, beyond which the battle to save Opperman's life was being fought.

Bubby Jones, clad in a purple Speedway Motors T-shirt and faded Levis, slipped into the adjacent chapel to kneel beside Mary Opperman (Jan's wife), Johnny Coogan, and the Leavells. All through the evening the in and out migration continued . . . drivers, mechanics, photographers, fans . . . people who either knew Jan or simply admired him.

Perhaps the saddest visitor of all was young James McElreath. Only twenty-two years of age, and already an excellent driver, his face readily revealed the sorrow felt for a close friend. Few of us could imagine it, but James was, himself, doomed. In a little over a year, he would be dead — the victim of another hideous, Indiana racing crash.

Finally, an official announcement regarding Jan's condition was made. Deeply unconscious and suffering from shock, the medical verdict proclaimed a severe cerebral contusion to be the most serious injury. Also, there was some paralysis which was believed to be temporary. But most significantly, his life signs were stabilizing.

As one doctor put it early the next morning . . . "Jan really had his bell rung, the blow to his head punched a nice hole in it and shook up his brain at the same time. The part of the brain involved is that part which keeps him awake. It isn't functioning because of the shock sustained, but after some rest it'll go to work again and Jan will wake up."

Within a few days, the physician's prophecy had been proven correct. "Opp" began thrashing around and soon he was awake for short periods of time. Gradually the periods of consciousness became longer in duration and, although there was some difficulty in recognizing certain people, he carried on conversations.

"His memory wasn't too good at first and his speech was slurred but Jan surely did want to talk," Mary Opperman remembers.

Nearly five weeks of rehabilitative therapy followed. "They had to teach me to move around, talk and think again . . . I told those doctors they couldn't do much for my thinking — 'cause it had never been any good," Jan says jokingly today.

At long last, Opperman's condition was deemed sufficiently improved to permit him out-patient status. "Mary, my Mom, two of my kids, and I went up to Rich Leavell's house in Elwood, Indiana," Opp explains. "Rich and Queenie were really great — they're truly hooked up with God. Whew, you should've seen me — what a mess — tryin' to walk around Rich's yard. Just like some strung-out junkie . . . staggering and stumbling. But I got better fast and soon I was out doing some slow jogging. When I felt strong enough Rich drove us all home to Noxon, Montana. Those old Rocky Mountains sure looked good."

Good or not, Jan Opperman was headed for a rough time . . . some agonizing days lay ahead. Rebuilding damaged reflexes, recovering lost strength, his racing future hanging in the balance . . . still "Opp" never complained. At least, never to me. "I'm alive, I've got my family and some wonderful friends — Praise God," he was and is fond of saying.

On several occasions since the time of the brutal accident that nearly snuffed out his life, Jan and I have discussed the incredible events of that day.

"Hey brother, you were there — right in the middle of that hassle; you gotta tell me something," he requested. "Was I dead — did I die out there in that dirt?"

"I can't say, not being a medical expert," I replied. "You surely looked dead, everyone thought so. If you weren't, then you couldn't have been far from it. Even a doctor thought you were a D.O.A."

"Yeah, I have talked to other guys who saw me and they say the same thing," Jan commented. "Bud Miller (a famed race promoter) and Coogan both said I looked like some dead animal that had just been shot by a hunter.

"So I have to believe the crash got me," he continued. " 'The Man' wasn't mad at me or anything like that; death isn't dealt out as a punishment. It's just that old Opperman had run one race too many — I was a goner. Then God heard all those good, country people praying for me. He felt all that love. He saw a bunch of hard-bitten characters, who had never believed in anything, tryin' to believe.

"Hey, let me tell you — there's no miracle about it. God doesn't need miracles . . . he can do anything he likes. In this situation he just changed his mind."

Eighteen months after the '76 Hoosier Hundred came to an abrupt halt on lap fifty-two, Jan Opperman was struggling up the steep hill to a racing comeback. He doesn't kid himself, he knows it's a rough trail. Still there is no bitterness in Jan's heart — none of the expected "why me" routine.

"Feel sorry for myself, I suppose I could," Opperman reflects quietly. "My career was given a severe setback, my financial status worse than that. But there is another side to the coin . . . a positive side. A lot of people shared in a powerful experience because of my accident and some of them became more inclined to believe — more inclined to be better Christians. Don't forget, I've been a minister for a number of years, as well as a racer. For the racer part of me the deal was a disaster; for the minister part a ton was gained. Gettin' hurt like I did was worth ten million or more of my words and there is no way I can be bitter toward something that may help a few folks find a little faith.

"The accident was a small price to pay for all that," he nods with a smile. "Besides, I'm a better person for it. Not a better racer, maybe, but a far better man. More humble, more appreciative, more grateful for the things that I do have. Also, I have been given the chance to practice what I preach as a loser — I had been a winner for a long time. I say that in a material sense; nobody is a loser if he gives himself to Jesus Christ."

Quite likely, such thoughts explain why we have chosen to begin our book with these two chapters — one about a ghastly accident and the other dealing with that accident's dramatic aftermath. For Jan Opperman truly feels that he was born again amidst the horror of a gut-tearing racing crash — the violence of which seemed bent on smashing the last bit of life from him.

The Best Place To Raise Kids

Watching Jan Opperman "pour the coal" to a wild-bucking Sprint Car* has been a mind-boggling experience these past ten years. SLAM . . . full throttle into a wheel-cleaved, corner ledge; SWOOSH . . . tearing through a hub-deep cushion, surrounded by a choking wall of flying dirt; sometimes sideways, sometimes air-borne — Opperman's drives have usually been classic examples in dirt tracking artistry. The sort of stuff from which racing legendry is traditionally manufactured.

Yet there is another angle to the Jan Opperman saga. Oddly enough, it has no relationship to the world of mud-caked helmets, racing gloves, or end over end, cart-wheeling nightmares. Long before he was old enough to realize that automobiles were actually raced against each other, Jan was a child of the mountains. Rugged, high country mountains — in his case only one range will do — The Rockies. To this very day Jan has remained a mountain man — living there when he was able, wishing he could when he wasn't.

Employing the vernacular of the blue-denimed set,

*Sprint Cars will need no introduction to racing fans. But for those people less versed on the subject they are open-cockpit machines, whose reputation is the most sinister in racing. Many a maimed driver and bereaved widow can attest to that. Slightly smaller in size than Champ-Dirt Cars, their power to weight ratio is the zaniest in all motorsport. Much more will be said of these four-wheeled titans of the half miles in later chapters.

Opperman's polarized mode of living is "mind blowing". On the one hand, we have this "foot to the floor" racer, whose Kamikaze-like charges have left many a grandstand tenant breathless and on the verge of heart failure. On the other, there is the matter of a peace-loving gent who craves the solitude of lonely logging camps, the smell of tall spruce clearings and the sound of fast-flowing trout streams.

"What's this thing you have with the mountains?" I once asked him.

"When you're trampin' around those parts you can really get hooked up with the land," he replied. "There is nothing phoney or fake about mountain places or mountain people . . . nothing to mess your head up either. Guess it was just the way I was raised that started it all."

Figuratively speaking, Jan first saw the light of day a long way from the Rocky Mountain style of life he adores. Jim and June Opperman's oldest son was born February 9, 1939 in Westwood Village, a suburb of Los Angeles, California. Just in case you haven't frequented the L.A. scene recently, let me acquaint you with Westwood. It is a compact little community that is best known for a couple of things — one being the home of The University of California at Los Angeles (UCLA) and two, a close proximity to the posh residential area of Beverly Hills. Westwood, and its residents, are totally into the Southern California syndrome, and if there are any mountaineer types around, they are strictly of the weekend variety. No doubt, the same circumstance prevailed when the Oppermans lived there, so long ago.

"Yeah, I was born in Westwood but we moved out right away," Opperman relates. "My dad was typical of a lot of men then and now . . . torn between makin' good money and livin' where they want. Most times the two don't go together.

"Anyway, Dad was (and still is) one of those restless types . . . California had the big jobs but he missed home. Both he and Mom had grown up near Spokane (Washington) and that's pretty mountainous country.

"One day they just loaded up and headed for the open

spaces. They went clear up into the Panhandle of Idaho and settled near the town of Bonners Ferry. Some of my best days were spent there.

"Wow, what a place," Jan remembers, with a twinge of nostalgia etched into his words. "It was a total wilderness . . . nothin' to do but fish and hunt. My brother (Jay) and I really loved it — hunting and fishing were right down our alleys. Dad insisted we do both to put meat on the table but he was wasting his breath. Jay and I would have done one or the other, no matter what.

"We were poor — real poor — or at least that's what the folks said. Me . . . I didn't know poor from rich . . . I was just a mountain kid. Today I know the truth about those times. I was rich . . . richer than anybody had a right to expect. There was a problem for Dad, however. Way out in the sticks like that, work was scarce. The only employment was in the loggin' business — everybody up there was a logger. Dad was no different, he muscled one of those big loggin' trucks over the dirt and gravel roads to make some money. It would have been all right but the weather played heck with the whole operation. There were just too many days when everyone and everything was snowed in."

For a moment, Jan Opperman paused in his reminiscing to ponder some recently recovered thought from yesterday. "Funny how simple things seem when you're a kid — sure is funny," he mused sadly.

"Well, back to the weather at Bonners Ferry — that's the reason we finally left there. I can remember Dad cryin' the blues about how poor we were . . . how he had to find a better job. Eventually he hired on with a long-haul trucking outfit (L.A. — Seattle Truck Lines) and we moved again. The move wasn't so bad because we settled on a little farm near Mount Rainier in Washington. That was nice country, also — lots of big timber, a beautiful river nearby, and plenty of hunting and fishing opportunities.

"There were two bad sides to our life at the Rainier place," Jan notes. "First of all, Dad was gone so much . . . long-haul truckers always are. We missed him, bein' as our family was real close and always did loads of things together. Secondly, he spent all of his time driving up and down the length of California. He couldn't help but see all that prosperity — all that so-called good life. I suppose it was only a matter of time, 'til Dad would have to try the California thing just once more. But that's another story, we're talking about mountains here."

At the present time, as my pencil scratches out these words, Jan Opperman hopes that he has returned to the Rocky Mountains for good. Several years ago, well fortified with race winnings, Jan began buying a piece of property near Noxon, Montana. Noxon, incidentally, is about a hundred miles from nowhere and that is precisely where "Opp" prefers his place of residence to be.

Surrounded by the vastness of The Kootenai National Forest, the Opperman homestead lies within an area that is steeped in the lore of Western Americana. Chief Joseph and his beleaguered Nez Perce warriors, attempted to take refuge in this trackless territory during their futile 1877 war with the United States Cavalry. Even before that, the rugged Bitter Root district was "the stomping ground" for some of American Folklore's most picturesque characters . . . the famed free trappers or Mountain Men, as they are usually referred to by historians. John Coulter, Davey Jackson, and the notorious "Liver Eating" Johnson were probably the first white men to feel the lure of high country living in that part of Montana. They, and assorted fellow members of the loner fraternity, trapped beaver in the icy streams, breathed the clear, brittle air, and generally resisted progress to the best of their abilities.

Looking at Jan Opperman, you have to wonder if that spirited breed ever really died out. His long hair and longer sideburns, faded Levis, lumberjack shirts, fringed moccasins and weathered Western Hat — surely there must be one last Mountain Man roaming the Bitter Roots.

"Can't say that I'd want to trap for a living or eat raw liver either," Opperman comments with a laugh. "But we do live pretty close to nature. All of our heating and cooking is done with wood . . . plenty of axe work up in Noxon. There are bears and cougars all around . . . sometimes they come in around the house.

"You know, although we live in Montana, our home isn't too far from Bonners Ferry, Idaho . . . about eighty miles. Guess I never forgot the thrill of being a kid in such a place. The country — especially mountain country — is the best place to raise kids. There is no doubt about that. I can only hope my four kids will benefit as I did from growin' up in a natural world. Although three of them are girls, they're into big trees, clean land, animals and fishin' just like their shaggy old man."

Jan Opperman knows all too well the wisdom of his words. As he drifted into adulthood, Jan dealt himself generous portions of trials and tribulations. Long before there was any guidance from the Christian ideal, values learned while living in the Rocky Mountains held him together. Always there was the dream of going back — in both fact and spirit. At last, he is home.

So when he came to the parting
Where one road led to the throne
And one went off to the mountains
And into the wild unknown,

He took the one to the mountains.

And there in a precipice valley
A girl of his age he met
Took him home to her bower,
Or he might have been running yet.

Lines from:
Robert Frost's THE BEARER OF EVIL TIDINGS.

California Kids Were Different

When Jan was sixteen years old and Jay but thirteen and a half, their father was bitten by the California fever for the last time. Having lived in a truck night and day, with little financial gain to show for his effort, the elder Opperman decided a change was in order. A friend of his was in the automobile business which — like everything else — was booming in California, at that time. Jim dreamed of owning his own used car lot and corraling some of the free-floating bucks that seemed to be eagerly awaiting someone (anyone) to snatch them from the sun-filled skies.

Consequently, the Oppermans relocated their address once again. They traded in "the high-lonesome" tranquility of Mount Rainier for a new start in the throbbing, urbanized society that makes up the San Francisco Bay Area. In their case, they settled on the East side of the Bay near Hayward.

California circa 1955 . . . what a place, especially for teenagers. Years ahead of its time, the whole state seemed to be undergoing an adolescent cultural shock wave of immeasurable magnitude. Drive-in parking lots crammed full of miniature James Deans, streets quaking with the sound of torqued-up hot rods, and everywhere there was the pulsating beat of the newly-discovered rock music — from San Francisco to Chula Vista the great youth movement was underway. "Cool" was the order of the day — everyone was "cool" and if you weren't, you soon learned to be.

Lurking in the distance, like an ominous fog bank off San Mateo Beach, lay harder times . . . psychedelic mania, Haight-Ashbury, the so-called Hippie movement, mass protesting and the awesome temptation of hard drugs. Far too often — in the silver screen manner of their idol (Dean) — California kids and their nationwide imitators were "Rebels Without a Cause". Not that there weren't causes available — plenty of them existed, but frequently they were too hazy in definition for the average finger-snapping devotee of the Elvis Presley sound and spinner hub caps.

Into that cataclysmic generation's domain shuffled Jan Opperman, wearing his backwoods upbringing in plain view for even the weakest pair of eyes to see. Twenty-three years later Jan's memories of the experience are still less than pleasant.

"California kids were really different than anything I'd ever seen," he recalls. "Real 'bee-boppie', toe-tappin' types . . . everyone trying to be so cool, so tough and so like each other. There I was — a genuine hick — with my Levis rolled up, lumberjack boots and faded flannel shirts. Hey brother, those guys thought I was just as strange as I believed them to be. The thing was — there were just two Oppermans and so many of those California dudes.

"That's when it all started. They began hassling me. Fightin' was big around there . . . the coolest characters were good fighters — or so they figured. Apparently they thought they could punch me right back to the 'boonies'. Well . . . they were in for a big surprise."

Jan Opperman can't help but smile while relating the details of that surprise. "Mountain kids are tough, especially this mountain kid," he chuckles. "I grew up around loggin' camps where fightin' was the religion. Not only that, but Dad (by the way we always call him 'Grizz') had been a professional fighter. He was undefeated in the pros and really on the move up the ladder until he got tired of beating people's brains out for money. Still he loved boxing for the sport of it and he taught me everything he knew. Ever since I was three years old, I had been wearing boxing gloves and I soon knew how to use them and the fists inside. One year up in Washington, I nearly won the state Golden Gloves Title. An older and more experienced fighter decisioned me in the championship bout.

"So when those California characters wanted to work me over, I was more than happy to 'punch their lights out' — that's what it was all about. They were 'duck soup' — easy pickings for someone with my background. Pretty soon I had whipped all the locals, but my reputation had spread. Then the fighters started showin' up, clear from San Francisco, to hunt me down. Some of those guys were crazy. You could punch them right down — right flat on their faces . . . they would lay there bleedin' and moanin' and then get up and beg to go again.

"Then there was Jay . . . he was younger and a little smaller than I. Next the local tough guys went to work on him. What a mistake — Jay was a better athlete than I . . . not only that he was a lot meaner and tougher. What he did to the boys was brutal — just brutal. Jay was a pure stud all the way.

"The worst part of the whole mess was that I half way liked it," Opperman frankly admits. "I was turned-on to violence . . . thinking fighting was good — boy, was I screwed up in those days.

"Anyway, eventually Dad got fed up with Jay and me. He never wanted us to get shoved around but neither did he teach us boxing to assist us in becoming street brawlers and thugs. Dad was all for ring fighting and I was still involved with that to some extent. Just not enough to please my father.

"Then one day I took stock of things and what I saw was mostly bad. Besides fighting there was all sorts of crud goin' on . . . stealing, gangs . . . plenty of stealing. I'd seen some of those early hippies and was amazed at their gentleness. They didn't fight, they didn't go around hurtin' people . . . they were on a different trip. To me, the hippie idea seemed to offer a pleasant alternative to my way of living. So I went that way

— started smokin' dope and bein' mellow toward everything. It was quite a change — a lot of people were shocked, but Jan Opperman, the skull-crunching fist fighter, was gone for good."

Looking back on that period of his life, Jan isn't suggesting the use of drugs to curb a violent nature. "Quite to the contrary," he says. "Drugs are bad — no doubt about that. Violence is defeated by love — not pills, grass, or anything in that category. But you have to study my actions within the time slot in which they happened. I was just a kid who realized his wrong direction . . . the peace and love folks seemed to have the answer to my problem. Their program was on the right track . . . you should care for and share your blessings with others. However, the use of dope to obtain that frame of mind — the phony spiritual cults — all of that was wrong. I see both the good and bad now. Consequently, I've tried to make use of the hippie good points and throw away the bad. After all, that's what growing up is all about — you should learn something in twenty or so years."

Through all that has followed, Jan Opperman's fists have remained conspicuously quiet. "You get mad racing; it's very easily done," he will tell you. "Especially in Sprint Cars where accepted tactics lead to plenty of wheel and car contact. I've yelled at a few guys but to actually slug a man . . . yeah, I do remember one time. Over at Williams Grove there was and is this particular driver. He liked to run into other people, using their cars as a cushion in the corners. He crashed me several races in a row . . . so, I knocked him flat on his back. It was either that or the dude was going to make history out of me. I'm not necessarily proud of what I did, but it was better than using my race car to nail him, (which I could have done.) A sore jaw beats a broken neck any day of the week. As I said, that driver is still around and he still does his roughneck thing . . . to other people, that is. He never bothered me again."

Stop being mean, bad-tempered and angry. Quarreling, harsh words, and dislike of others should have no place in your lives. Instead, be kind to each other, tenderhearted, forgiving one another. *Ephesians 4:31, 32*

Motorcycles And Slippery Streets

Jan Opperman — looking back at his teen-age years in California — describes himself as a "Mean Mother of an Outlaw". Maybe so, but every penny has two sides — even supposedly bad ones.

In all the hullabaloo about hippies, drugs and street fighting, it is often overlooked that Jan was a superb high school football player. He played quarterback, and in the vernacular of those of us who follow the game, he had a "major league arm". For sure, his ability to zero-in on pass receivers with bullet-like throws, seemed destined to carry him a long way . . . perhaps south again to Westwood and UCLA.

No matter the future — Jan approached football as he has every phase of his life . . . plunging his heart and soul all the way to the hilt with each effort. He was a sixty minute player who insisted upon doubling as a linebacker on defense. One day, after a particularly bone-jarring tackle, Jan got to his feet clutching a shattered right shoulder. Extensive surgery could not repair the damage, and the golden throwing arm's potential was lost forever. A great, jagged scar (clearly visible these many years later) adorns Jan's shoulder in lasting memorial to a young quarterback, whose love for the game wouldn't allow him to take it easy when his team was on defense.

"It was sad but it was my fault," Jan notes, unconsciously rubbing the injury. "I would like to have tried college ball . . . quarterback was my chance — but I loved that linebacking.

As it turned out, no college wanted a quarterback who couldn't throw and I was a little small for a big-time linebacker. Yet everything works out for the best. I became a racer and that was, no doubt, what God intended for me to be. The Lord operates in strange ways."

No doubt about that . . . Jan Opperman seems to have been born to the sport of speed. He was a natural in any high-winding vehicle and that skill first manifested itself in motorcycle racing. Before he had graduated from high school, "Opp" was racing professional American Motorcycle Association (AMA) bikes over the half mile and mile-long dirt ovals that constituted the merciless Pacific Coast flat-track circuit.

"Motorcycles (or motorsickles, as Jan calls them) were the hot items those days in California," Opperman relates. Everybody loved them and I loved them more than most. We rode 'em on the streets and when we got brave enough we raced 'em on the wild dirt tracks.

"I shouldn't tell you this, you bein' an old school teacher — but I will. The rainy days . . . how we would wait for those rainy days. When it rained all of us crazies would either skip school or sneak out of school to get our bikes onto the wet streets. Man, we'd haul those big 'forty inchers' or whatever, over that slippery pavement . . . slidin' the corners, feelin' all that power spinnin' beneath you. Bad stuff — well, I guess. It was just a way of life . . . some guys got hurt and we should have been in school. As I said, we were crazy.

"For me, the serious racin' began during my senior year in high school. The Bay Area was particularly a hotbed for flat-track bikers. Some of AMA's best riders lived and raced extensively in those parts . . . people like Joe Leonard, Dick Mann and Dick Dorresteyn.* They are some of the classy

*Joe Leonard achieved three AMA National titles in his career (1954, 1956, 1957). He won a total of twenty-seven AMA National Races and went on to auto racing greatness. Dick Mann was twice AMA National Champion (1963, 1971) and owns twenty-four National victories. Dick Dorresteyn, on the other hand, confined his activities primarily to West Coast events. He did claim two top-ten point finishes (seventh in 1958 and eighth in 1959) and two National Circuit triumphs (Peoria, Ill. in 1958 and Gardena, California, in 1962).

characters that I ran against," Jan notes, shaking his head.

"Those guys, and the others, were super racers . . . they could have raced anyone in anything. Look how good Leonard became in cars. But of them all, it was Dorresteyn that really blew me away. I know that Dick Dorresteyn is hardly a household name most places . . . other bikers gathered up more fame. Around there, however, he was a legend and even the famous ones knew it. When you were on the track with him you really got an education . . . a hard, tough racer, for sure.

"How much do you know about bike racin'?" Jan asked me during our conversation about his beginnings in that segment of motorsport.

"Not really too much," I replied. "I've seen a few races and it scares me to death."

"O.K., I'm going to tell you something that you may find hard to believe," he continued. "Motorcycle racers are, in my opinion, the fiercest racers of all — and I mean fiercest. That goes for cars, boats, Indianapolis, Sprint Cars . . . you name it. They're just plain racier, they travel in a dimension that's hard to believe. Everything is so finely cut; the margin for error is nearly zero. Take a mile dirt track for example — you blow down the straightaways at a hundred miles an hour, then lay the bike over in the turns, stick your leg out and slide through. Praise God, if you fall. You truly have to be dialed-in with the system, because, if not, you'll become well acquainted with various hospital staffs. It's easy to spot a biker . . . chain scars, a pair of gimpy legs and a body that resembles a medical catastrophe quickly identifies him."

As each of us knows, Jan Opperman eventually turned away from the motorcycles, and their murderous propensity for maiming, to concentrate on the four-wheelers. With very little experience, once he got the opportunity, Jan quickly zoomed to auto racing prominence. His rapid acceleration within the field amazed many a grizzled veteran of the steering wheels-only faction. "Opp" explains it this way.

"It goes back to what I said previously . . . motorcycle competition is fierce competition. You learn a lot and you had better learn it quickly. It's especially good training for dirt tracking . . . how to miss the holes, judging the best racing groove, when and where to pitch it for the turns . . . things like these are necessities for a biker. Not just to win, but to keep on breathin'.

"Sure I moved up fast in dirt track race cars. Why not . . . I had received my training in the toughest company. Chasing after super dudes like Dick Dorresteyn."

As free spirited a soul as Opperman was (and still is) he never really fit in with the motorcycle crowd. Joe Scalzo, the renowned author of numerous auto and motorcycle racing selections, discusses that phenomenon in his classic Sprint Car book, "Stand on the Gas".

"One biker of that period, Ralph White, recalls that Opperman 'was a little weird'. Meaning that while other riders took part-time jobs in motorcycle shops during the winter, weird Jan Opperman, a nonconformist already, toiled as a blacksmith, making horseshoes.

"He was too tall, too muscular to be a biker anyway; when he crashed (and he had dozens of gory crashes), Jan usually broke something and even his swollen muscles didn't stop him from being laid up for long periods of time.*

Setting aside "the weird" diagnosis and the drug and street brawling raps, Jan Opperman had made quite a mark for himself by high school graduation day. In three of the highest risk games around — boxing, football and professional motorcycle racing — the kid from the logging country had earned his stripes. Yet the greatest days were still over the horizon . . . off toward the point of sunrise and the ever-deadly speed cathedrals at such revered locations as Knoxville (Iowa), Terre Haute, Williams Grove (Pennsylvania) and, of course, Indianapolis.

*Joe Scalzo, **Stand on the Gas** p.75, Prentice Hall, Inc. (Englewood Cliffs, N.J. 1974)

An Old V8-60 and A Girl Named Mary Lou

Somewhere during the break between the '61 and '62 biking seasons, Opperman turned away from motorcycle racing. As a replacement for the chain-driven machines, he turned toward a long-time dream of his — race cars.

"Scalzo is right," Jan says. "I was too big for a biker and I was hurt too much, as well. One of my kidneys was destroyed ridin' the "motors" plus my carcass had been pretty well scuffed up. Anyway, my goal had always been to get into race cars.

"Cars, fast-running cars, had nearly always fascinated me. I'd been drivin' alone since I was nine . . . going to town for groceries and so forth. Had my own car when I was twelve and drove it to school many a day. At that time, you could get away with this kind of thing in the far-out places where we lived.

"Plenty of my raciness came from Dad," Jan chuckles. "He was just an old hot rodder, himself. He'd take me out into a field and show me how to slide a car in the dirt . . . man, that tore me up. Not only that, what roads we had were covered with snow and ice much of the time — so slidin' a car was an important fact of our lives. I didn't know much about real race cars but if the chance ever came, I was ready to learn.

"When we moved to Washington, I got a better street car. Those country kids around Rainier drove like madmen. I have to laugh when people talk about country kids . . . you know, how good they're supposed to be. They're good 'cause few cops are around to prove them otherwise.

"I'm ashamed to say but Opperman was right out there with them . . . the maddest of the mad. I was too stupid to realize that cars were and are death dealers. Today, it makes me shudder to think of the stuff we did . . . the kids that got wasted, the insanity of it all. Runnin' The Indianapolis 500 is a far safer proposition than bein' the local hot rod hero. The only good thing about it was that it did give me some high-speed drivin' experience for becoming a genuine race driver," he concludes.

In the months that followed Jan's switch in motorsport direction, he started hanging around the tracks that featured Midget Car* competition as provided by the Bay Cities Racing Association. These were hard times for "Oppie". Week after week he waited at the various pit gates, carrying his battered helmet, trying to land a ride in one of the little dynamos. No dice . . . Jan's reputation had arrived well ahead of him. He was judged a prime example of those new Hippie types, smoked that marijuana junk and even the crazy bikers thought him to be weird and too reckless. Bad enough that he had torn up a sizable number of motorcycles . . . he wasn't going to be handed the opportunity to do a similar number on someone's Offy Midget.

Consequently, further turned off by the system, Opperman retreated deeper within the hippie movement. From time to time, he disappeared altogether . . . drifting off into the creepy mists of the Santa Cruz Mountains to smoke some dope and ponder his plight. When his spirit was replenished, he would start showing up at the tracks again. A hippie he was . . . peace and love had his blessing . . . but he was a hard-nosed gent when it came to quitting.

*Again, for the non-race oriented reader, Midgets are the smallest of the oval track, open-cockpit vehicles. Nonetheless, they are potent items that have been the training ground for some of America's greatest race drivers. In Jan's early years the hot setup was a Kurtis chassis powered by a 110 cubic inch Offenhauser motor — a miniature version of the powerplant then dominating Indianapolis Car Racing.

"There was a hassle — tons of hassle — in 'them days' ". Jan recollects, his obvious bitterness prompting a return to lumber camp grammar. "Those BCRA guys thought they had me pegged . . . a real no-good, who had no business in their equipment.

"Sure I had no experience in cars, but what they didn't realize — or wouldn't admit — was that, as a biker, I had raced in spheres of speed that even many of their best drivers had never known. I knew I could drive those things — absolutely, I knew I could.

"I don't mean to cut down the BCRA drivers. There were some fantastic racers among them — namely Dick Atkins.* Too bad he had to get killed. Believe me — I would never hang a bum tag on any bunch of racing folks, but surely you can understand my frustration. Right then and there I decided I'd had it with California . . . good things weren't happening to me there. Just as soon as I could figure where to go and how to get there . . . I was gonna leave. There was obviously no place for me in California racing circles . . . being so green I just didn't know what was happening other places."

1965 saw Jan Opperman finally get his chance. The car was old, the motor of yesterday's vintage, but chances were few and far between. Jan's words tell the tale best.

"The chassis was old but sanitary. The motor was one of the old Ford V8-60 powerplants — once very popular in Midgets. Essentially that's a stock engine which had to run against Offenhausers. The Offies might be hurtin' in today's racing . . . then they were unbeatable. No way could a V8-60 eat those fire-breathin' Offies on a regular basis.

"But I crawled into that little car and drove it for all both of us were worth. Over a period of time, I won some heats and made most main events. I never won a main . . . usually we finished about seventh or eighth behind a pack of Offenhausers.

*Atkins was fatally injured, along with Don Branson, in a grinding 1966 Sprint Car accident at Gardena, California. At that time he had cracked the big time and was probably considered the brightest hope for future stardom in American auto racing.

"I thought I was doin' O.K., however the BCRA people weren't convinced," Opperman laments. "They were positive that I was totally insane, clear over my head and driving way too hard for my experience. Most of them were really spooked by my tactics on the track . . . really spooked. He's gonna kill himself or the dope makes him brave . . . such were the heavy opinions laid on me.

"Neither was true. I had no intention of killing myself and never — I repeat, never — did I mix dope and racing. You know me, I'm an honest man . . . I've never tried to hide my mistakes. Dope and racing — that never was my trip.

"The truth was a simple thing. Drivin' Midgets was so easy compared to what I'd been through in motorcycles . . . cars, with those four wheels under me, seemed like duck soup. Sometimes I think the BCRA characters just got blown away when they saw an old Ford 60 beat some of their Offenhausers. It was more easily explained when the Ford 60 driver was labeled a crazy, brainless hippie who got his courage from a bag of grass.

"I'm older now and I can better understand how they may have felt about me," Jan adds sincerely. "A different dude comes down the road and he creates instant suspicion. Back then I was mad and became more determined than ever to pull out of California for good — the sooner the better."

Tough or not, '65 was a big year for Jan Opperman. His career in automobile racing was at last in motion and it was during that spring that he first met Mary Lou. Like Jan, she was not a "true-blue" Californian — having moved there from the black-ground corn country of Iowa. This quiet, uncommonly-pretty girl from the Midwest was to present one of the more positive influences in Jan's turbulent life.

"Opp" had long been a hard-core ladies' man . . . girls were strongly attracted to him and vice versa. He had been married once but the marriage had failed. Jan has never offered any excuses for that failure.

"We were too young — we were wrong for each other and what can you say," he confesses. "I was no bargain . . . off racin', doin' the hippie thing and — yes — chasin' all the stray chicks. One thing about it was good . . . we had a daughter, Teacia. For a long time we were apart, but Teacia is sixteen now and we're together most of the time. Teacia and I are real close — great pals."

Then came Mary Lou — a gal who was cut a bit differently than most female types Jan had run across. The relationship launched a marriage that has lasted for twelve years — a solid, substantial, caring thing that certainly has helped to mold the Jan Opperman of today.

"Jan and I met on a blind date in June of 1965," Mary relates. "I might not have known him before, but I certainly had heard about him . . . everyone had heard about the Opperman Brothers. They were rather notorious around the area . . . sort of the super jocks of the town.

"Jan had only driven one Midget race when I met him. I had never seen any kind of a race at that time. He let me know from the very start that racing was his thing, so I best like it or not get involved. Anyway, I grew to love racing then and still do.

"My parents weren't crazy about racing or Jan at first. But soon they came to love him just as I did. It's hard not to love Jan Opperman . . . there's something so appealing about him.

"My brother once called him a 'thrill seeker' . . . that always makes me laugh," and Mary Lou smiles in that special way of hers. "Our life has definitely been a constant thrill . . . there is nothing dull about my husband. He's the most exciting person I've ever known or hope to know."

For a moment Mary Lou Opperman paused in her commentary to brush aside her long brown hair. "I would like to make one point about Jan," she continued. "He has always been a fascinating character — one who plunged his whole self into everything that involved him. Good or bad . . . Jan has consistently given his all — there is nothing half way about June and Jim Opperman's oldest son. Lots of people have misjudged him, but I see that as their fault. Jan tells the truth, conceals nothing and presents no phony front . . . he is himself at all times. I love him for being just Jan Opperman."

Listening to this discussion, Jan sucked in his breath and whispered a reply. "Mary, you old trophy girl, you're gettin' old and sentimental."

Then he looked my way and clearly made his point. "Along with Christ, Mary and my kids have been my whole strength. Mary has been everything to me . . . before she came into my life I was headed nowhere. With her — together — we have made something beautiful. She is love and courage . . . she even produces the memory for my scrambled-up head. She is just the best, she is . . . oh well, I can't say it any better."

And this maiden she lived with no other thought
  Than to love and be loved by me.
She was a child and I was a child,
  In this kingdom by the sea.
But we loved with a love that was more than love —
  I and my Annabel Lee —
With a love that the winged seraphs of Heaven
  Coveted her and me.

Edgar Allen Poe's *Annabel Lee*

The Psychedelic Trip

For years, people (writers, newspapermen and just the curious) have questioned Jan Opperman concerning his admitted use of drugs. How he got involved, how he got off them — all the gruesome details have been eagerly ferreted out. Doing so has never been difficult, as Jan has frankly discussed his problem with all who desired to listen.

"It's my duty . . . I was sorely deceived and people — especially kids — should know about it," Jan concedes. "Drugs are a crutch — an escape trip — and that's wrong. I don't believe God intends for us to always be continually escaping. Crutches cheat you — they interfere with your ability to face things . . . chiefly what you are or what you aren't. It doesn't matter whether you're talkin' about dope, booze, sex or even racing. I know some guys who limp through life using racing as a crutch. So let my mistakes be out in the open . . . somebody might learn something."

Several times in preceding chapters of this book, Jan and drugs have been mentioned. Because of the topic's importance, this entire section's contents will be devoted to the issue. Appropriately, "Opp's" own words shall carry the ball.

"Let's go back to my fighting days," he remarks. "I was feared, respected — a regular right-on dude. Then, as I said earlier, I got sick of it. I realized I'd been living a lie — a whole bunch of lies. Beatin' guys up wasn't my thing and I wanted out. To avoid hassles, I stopped going around at night and started hanging around the house — stayin' inside.

"All of my friends weren't red-necked alley brawlers — a couple of 'em were hippies. Shortly after I graduated from high school one of these mellow characters said to me, 'Hey Jan, you're tired of all the hostility, start smokin' grass and everything will get better.' So I began regularly puffin' on joints. In my messed up state, he seemed to be right. I became more compassionate, move loving . . . started lookin' into people's hearts instead of at their fists. Homely people even looked beautiful to me.

" 'Far out brother,' I said to myself. Dope is the salvation of the world — the real salvation of the world. I started preachin' the merits of grass to everyone . . . tryin' to turn 'em on to that salvation. I even worked at turnin' my parents on.

"Of course, you'll want to know what other drugs I tried. No heroin, no needle stuff . . . I was still too athletically oriented to get into anything like that. But I did experiment with LSD and other hallucinogenic crud . . . I was what was called a psychedelic freak. Except for the times when I was doing bike racing, I stayed plastered much of the time. Some of us would go up into the mountains, blow ourselves away and stay for days. Man, what a worthless trip.

"Still I was convinced that drugs were good. After all, they had converted me from a mean outlaw and thief to a warm, caring individual. Then I began to look around me . . . I saw kids (friends of mine) with their brains rotted away by acid — just vegetables. One day they'd be O.K., the next day they were gone. I saw others takin' speed or 'shooting-up' like crazy . . . cryin', sobbin', and shakin' all over. I thought to myself, 'Opperman, something is wrong here . . . something is clear haywire. If drugs are the salvation of the world . . . how can they be wreckin' all these lives?' The truth was plain enough — my life before drugs had been a lie but the drug deal was a lie too — just a different lie. Boy, was I confushed then.

"Do you know what is the worst thing about drugs?" he

once asked me, sadly. Before he could respond, he answered his own question. "They're bad enough for everyone, but too often the wrong people are in most deeply. Lonely, confused, weak and unstable types . . . they make the best hard druggers. The healthiest mind would have a tough time coping with dope . . . the messed-up minds explode. Yet, except for occasional flings at grass, it's the messed-up minds that seek refuge in the drug culture — not the jokers with their heads on straight.

"How did I survive . . . that's easy enough. I drew the line. Except for LSD my drug business centered around marijuana. I stayed pretty cool and level headed . . . for me drugs were a fad — that escape trip I talked about — nothing more.

"In the end it was my common sense that broke me away from all that. Salvation of the world — no way — there was the great deception. Plus, I had help — Mary Lou, my desire to be a car racer and, most of all, the discovery of Christ. I'm not saying that a drug user can't be a good Christian . . . I'll lay no judgments on anyone. There would come a time, however, when a choice would just have to be made. You can't give your soul to Jesus and then sell that same soul to the devil.

"Marijuana has been the hardest part of it for me to give up — I admit that. It has taken a long, long time, but God took me into his fold anyway. Remember, the Lord cleans his fish after he catches them. I won't say when I quit," Jan comments, "But I stopped the grass. Why . . . because I made a deal with God . . . no more crutch, he's my strength now.

"Besides, God says obey the laws of the land. Sure, there are folks who say the prohibition of pot is a foolish law. Probably it is . . . but God allows the laws to be made. He expects good Christians to obey them all, especially those that seem foolish. Any jerk can comply with a law that he agrees with or understands."

Interrupting Jan in his explanation, I questioned him about the Hippie Movement.

"Earlier you said the hippie idea had some good points — how about its drug connection?" I asked.

"Yeah, all the dope spooked many people away from hippies. It gave the whole concept a bad name. But don't forget, there was plenty more to bein' a hippie than using a lot of drugs.

"Hippie comes from the word hip, which means thinking straight, bein' tuned to a better life or having yourself together. The original hippies were thoroughly turned off by the things goin' on . . . senseless wars, selfishness, crookedness, brutal competition and all the lies bein' told by supposedly honest people. They stressed lovin' your neighbor instead of hating him, sharing, caring for the less fortunate, openness and truth . . . you know the things I'm talking about.

"I agreed with all that, I still do. My own life was the very proof of the bad things hippies argued against. So I joined them. I worked hard at the new philosophy . . . in all honesty I'm probably still one. As for the Hippie Movement, I was into that for ten years. Christianity is my movement today.

"The hippie deal got all screwed up, however," Jan frankly recognizes. "Everybody started imitating hippies or so they thought. Wearing long hair, patched clothes . . . even the so-called straight people tried to look like hippies, thinkin' it was cool. It turned into one big giant fad . . . loads of people were involved and most of them understood nothing about the original purposes. They talked about peace and love, used foul language, did the dope bit . . . yet the real meaning of the hippie spirit was overlooked.

"Take the Haight-Ashbury situation, as an example. I had connections there but rarely went into the district. That was just a bunch of people — kids mostly — who dressed and acted as freaky as possible. Their chief goal seemed to be directed at shocking all the straights . . . really shocking them. It was like a big carnival sideshow . . . all the regular dudes walkin' around staring at the freaks.

"I wore my hair long because I liked it that way and my old Levis . . . I wore them, because in the beginning I was too poor to have anything else. I had always worn old Levis, ever since the mountain days. Trying to look weird and way out . . . not me . . . different, but not weird and way out. The individuals who were on the weird trip — the Haight-Ashbury types — were playing games with the rest of society. What the heck, I became a hippie in order to stop playing games.

"In the end, the Hippie Movement died. Partly due to drugs, but not primarily. The big reason was that it became as phony as the very things it had opposed in the first place. The sincere guys pulled out to get away from this new fakery, and all the counterfeit hippies drifted away to new fads. Still, the fact remains — good ideas were there once. Ideas, I might add, very closely connected to the teachings of Christ."

As promised, Jan's dialogue relating to these difficult subjects has been allowed to flow freely, unencumbered by the comments of this writer. I know little about drugs and very little more that is pertinent to the hippie culture. That being in spite of the fact that "Opp" frequently refers to me as an old hippie. But Jan Opperman does know — all too well. Clearly his thoughts form the words to a very important axiom for dialed-in living: ***Most often the crutches that tempt us along life's rutted road, carry price tags that are way too high.***

Teach Me To Be A Hippie and I'll Take You Where The Racin' Is

Surely the gent that invented the sport of Sprint Car Racing must have done so from the padded confines of a mental institution. For there is nothing remotely sane about the things Sprint Cars, and the few who dare to drive them, are expected to do. Traditionally, they run on small tracks (usually a half mile or shorter) that are choked equally with swirling dust clouds and too many sideways — running competitors. Even the paved circuits, that occasionally appear on association schedules, offer little relief to men whose nerves ought to be frayed beyond repair, but seldom are.

With further reverence to traditionalism — Sprint cars have steadfastly clung to their well-earned reputation of being motorsport's most dangerous vehicles. Too heavy in the power department, too light in the chassis category — Sprinters seem possessed by some exotic form of automotive schizophrenia and are totally unpredictable. They leap and jump around a track (frequently into each other) with all the gusto of a cage full of hyperactive tigers. Because of this inherent unpredictability, Sprint Car events are generally short both in distance and duration. Hence the name Sprint arises . . . flat out, all out runs for glory that permit no holding back in either speed or bravery.

Steering a Sprinter into a mushy clay turn at eighty miles an hour is serious stuff and the man doing so had better treat the action accordingly. It's no secret that Sprint Cars are suicidally inclined mechanisms. With almost no provocation, they will stagger wildly into the deepest ruts, vault into the air and end over end it — until stopped by the nearest immovable object. Woe to the driver who experiences such a topsy-turvy, heart-stopping bit of horror (they all do, eventually), but it used to be worse. Before 1970, most Sprint Cars didn't have roll cages over their cockpits to protect defenseless drivers. In that time and before, helmeted heads too often contacted the upcoming ground before anything else. Consequently, on the days when Sprinters performed, ambulance drivers did a booming business. They don't do badly, even today, with roll cages a merciful and universal blessing.

Don't get me wrong, in my way, I love the ultimate brand of competition presented by Sprint Cars. But there is one significant aspect to that affection — I don't drive them. Jan Opperman loves Sprint Cars too (he calls them fire breathers) and he does drive them. Well that he feels this way, because in their raging, deafening world, peace-loving Jan has achieved unprecedented auto racing legendry.

Oddly enough, Opperman knew little of Sprint Car Racing until the late "Sixties". Northern California, his home area, was then hardly famous for its support of the violent game . . . Midgets and Motorcycles, yes — but Sprint Cars were frowned upon. Ironically, in that state's Southern sector — especially the Los Angeles area — the ferocious machines were unrivaled darlings of local speed sport enthusiasts. Jan — trapped by Bay Area provincialism and busy with his hippie business — chose not to explore the possibilities.

"How do you explain something like that?" Opperman questions in retrospect." I guess I just wasn't hip to the California racing scene, or any racing scene. I knew about Ascot Park* but I had just become so "bum-kicked" with

*Ascot Park, located in South Los Angeles County, at the intersection of the Harbor and San Diego Freeways, has for twenty-one years been a supreme proving ground for dirt track racers . . . especially those of the Sprint Car variety. Built on the site of an old garbage dump, Ascot turf provides a racing surface that is as lethally fast as any in the country.

California that its only assets seemed to be the hippie thing and plenty of pot to be had."

Sadly, Jan was to learn first hand of Ascot Park's potential for cruelty. With only a season or so of Sprint Car competition under his belt, he hauled into Ascot on April 13, 1968 for one of the weekly shoot-outs. During the program, his Sprinter unavoidably caromed off the out-of-control car driven by forty-one year old Hank Henry. "Opp's" machine flipped down the track. When it finally halted in its self-destructing journey, Opperman crawled from the debris, badly cut and dazed. Henry, one of the Southwest's most popular drivers and car builders, was not as fortunate. He was dead.

"When they told me Henry was gone, I wanted to throw my guts up — I bawled like a baby. Everyone said it wasn't my fault but all I could think about was that poor guy," Jan recalls, his voice cracking from the painful memory.

"It took a while to get myself hooked-up mentally with racing after that. You just have to understand that race cars — especially Sprints — can be fierce death dealers . . . they're just machines, they don't give a darn. Many times, I've felt sick that way, since the Henry deal . . . I've cried for plenty of torn up dudes, I'll tell you."

Turning away from that savage night at Ascot, allow me to flip the calendar back one year . . . to 1967 and Jan Opperman's initial success as a Sprint Car racer. Although he had taken several previous shots at the wicked four-wheelers, his greatest opportunity came in the autumn of '67.

"Hank Hanestead gave me my best chance," Jan quickly states. "Yup, old Hank Hanestead — he was a good ol' man. He had this Sprint Car . . . you should've seen it . . . what a beast. It was a big old, ugly old, handmade monster . . . everything on that car came from the junkyard. And get this, it had a Ranger* engine for power. Ugly and big and giant . . . but

*Rangers were enormous but rather lightly-weighted engines, that had been designed for airplanes. That's right — airplanes, which proves the point I made about the power situation in Sprint Cars. In the years after World War II they were popular items, but by 1967 the Ranger's role in auto racing had generally been relegated to history.

that ol' boy knew what he was doing. That car was fast . . . whew, I mean really fast.

"We took the beast car up to Vallejo for my first try with it and I won. I won big — really dusted 'em.

"Suddenly everything was different. Nobody said, 'hey Opperman, you're drivin' like an insane man' or 'you're way over your head'. Nobody said much about my hair, which was pretty shaggy by then, or dope. I was a hero . . . a regular, all-together racer. Everyone wanted to shake my hand or pat me on the back . . . man, what a change. Maybe it happened because I was a winner or maybe it was because the Sprint Car people were of a different breed than those BCRA Midget guys had been."

Talk about hitting the proverbial nail squarely on the head, Jan's above-stated analysis of his newly acquired popularity gets an A for accuracy. Almost everyone loves a winner . . . the losers usually face their defeats alone. More than that, he is correct in his surmise concerning Sprint Car folks. From the lowliest stooge to the most famous driver, the clan's total membership is afflicted with terminal fanaticism. All night tows, endless dollars spent, and pushing the howling machine to the front any way you can . . . these are the key symptoms in diagnosing severe cases of "Sprint Caritis".

Consequently, Sprint Car drivers' personal lives are seldom questioned by their associates. Neither are rowdy driving tactics, for the entire shrieking ritual is a rowdy, rugged happening. Of primary concern is the power in a man's throttle foot and the extent of his courage. At long last, Jan Opperman had found a home in auto racing.

Among the crowd of well wishers that gathered around Jan after his Vallejo win was a foot-loose Nebraskan, who, unknowingly, came to have a profound influence on Opperman's rising star.

"This guy walked up after the race," Jan recounts. "It was the craziest conversation you ever heard. He told me his name was Yogi Janson, that he was from Lincoln, Nebraska, and that he'd been a mechanic for Bill Smith.* Neither name meant anything to me. But then I didn't know anything about anything in those days.

"Then he put some words on me that I'll never forget. He said, 'Hey kid, you've really got it. You're wasting your time in Northern California . . . why don't you let me take you back where the real racin' is?' Yogi went on to tell me about the dozens of dirt tracks, fancy Sprinters and rich purses in the Midwest.

"Now those were just the words I had been waitin' to hear for a long time. This Yogi character seemed to have the ticket that I needed . . . some connections with authentic professional racers. Being so thoroughly disgusted with California, I told him I would go tomorrow or even tonight.

"However, that didn't end the deal. Yogi said he had a car but not a dime to his name . . . that I would have to pay for the gas plus other expenses on the way to Lincoln. That was no problem and I quickly agreed.

"Next he presented the weirdest proposition that I've ever heard — in or out of racing. 'Opperman, I really dig this hippie thing,' he told me, 'I'll take you back to Lincoln and set you up with some important racers, but first you gotta teach me to be a hippie.'

"Let me say, that really blew me away. Here was this straight dude from Nebraska — where they had probably never seen a hippie — wantin' me to teach him to be one. How do you teach someone to be a hippie, anyway? I laughed then and it still makes me laugh today. Still, I could see Yogi was dead serious and I sure did want to get to that super racing country. So I said, 'O.K. brother, I'll transform you into the fiercest hippie in these parts or any parts'."

Throughout the Winter and Spring of '67-'68 Jan Opperman drove Sprint Cars when possible and coached his

*Bill Smith has long been a power in Midwest auto racing. His Sprint Cars have always been among the fastest around and Opperman would eventually team with him for some fabulous victories. Smith's Speedway Motors Company is one of the largest suppliers of racing equipment in the country.

protege, Yogi Janson, in the proper style of hippie living. Jan also learned some important things during those same months — especially an ability to gag down the rancid taste of death after hideous disasters like the Hank Henry accident.

By the time the hot winds of summer were floating over the parched prairies to the East — Jan, his oldest daughter (Teacia), and Yogi were on their way to Nebraska.

"Numerous people will probably question my taking Teacia along on such an uncertain thing as that Nebraska trip," Jan acknowledges with a grin. "She was awful young — only six — but we really loved each other . . . in spite of the problems her Mom and I had known. She liked being with me and racing was already a part of her life. I have never understood drivers who don't want their family members around . . . I need the support of mine and they want to be near me when I'm working my trade. Teacia is sixteen now and she has covered many a mile over this country with her race car drivin' dad. Again, it goes way back to my childhood experiences . . . families should live the good and bad times together."

Whatever, one of the strangest business agreements in the annals of motorsport was about to be completed. Yogi Janson could classify himself a full-fledged hippie and Jan Opperman had taken the first step to auto racing greatness.

"Sprint Cars eat women, small children
and dogs for breakfast."

Joe Scalzo

Covered With Hay and Cobwebs

If a writer were so inclined, he or she could probably put together an entire volume on the Midwestern auto racing heritage. In fact, it is no small group of people, who will firmly defend its conviction that the best of American motorsport revolves about the rock-hard dirt tracks and asphalt-coated speed bowls, nearly hidden by seemingly endless fields of waving wheat and towering corn. Especially this is true when the subject of Sprint Car racing is brought forth.

The roots plunge deeply into that rich soil . . . clear to the memory of Percheron Horses, steam threshing engines, Barney Oldfield* and skinny, knobbed racing tires. Oldfield is long gone and so, for the most part, are Percheron Horses, but things really haven't changed all that much. Looking for excitement, today's Grain Belt residents still pack grandstands, on steamy summer nights, to watch helmeted daredevils prove the validity of an ancient agrarian theorem. That being, that well-engineered machinery can dominate the cantankerous nature of gumbo clay. Peering through eyes, permanently dust-blurred by the dawn to dusk toiling of John Deere diesels and Gleaner Combines — these rural people clearly recognize only the fiercest varieties of auto racing.

*In the dawning days of auto racing, Barney Oldfield helped to pioneer the barnstorming, open-cockpit brand of speed sport, still featured in the Midwest. Like many of his successors, Oldfield was a dirt track devotee.

Consequently, their heroes represent the fiercest variety of our race driving species.

Curiously, Midwestern racing (particularly Sprint Cars) is a blend of the smells of methanol fumes and corn dogs, the haunting look of hard-eyed men and the sounds of county fair midways harmonizing with two dozen high-winding engines. And, of course, there are the ghastly crashes . . . the rolling, tearing, tumbling crashes. Many a promising driving career has been seen vaulting into oblivion over a low, almost non-existent guard rail, or being pounded to pieces by a numberless repetition of repulsive flips. Yes, Sprint Car battles — mid-continent style — are real "blood and guts", "survival of the fittest" extravaganzas.

All of these "do or die" showdowns are staged by one or the other of two possible systems . . . either under the watchful eye of a racing association or via the loosely organized but always tough open competition route.

Among the associations, two have dominated the scene in recent years. First there is the United States Auto Club or USAC, as it is most frequently called. Heavily frosted with the prestige of having the sanctioning authority for the Indianapolis 500, USAC's haughty membership will proclaim its superiority to any and all listeners. In truth, the club's drivers are an extremely talented lot.

But to numerous wind-burned denizens of America's Heartland, USAC has meant very little. Chiefly because the organization's policy has never favored the so-called fair circuit as a showplace for its Sprint Car Division. Instead, that territory has been the property of IMCA (International Motor Contest Association). Going back to the era of World War I, the sun-battered horse tracks of the Great Plains country and Western Corn Belt have known very well the pounding wheels of IMCA's open-cockpit bravados. All of the promoters, making up the club's network, take great pride in discussing the names of now-famous Indianapolis 500 drivers who cut professional racing teeth beneath the IMCA banner. Parnelli Jones, Jim Hurtubise, Johnny Rutherford, Lee Kunzman and

— yes — Jan Opperman, are just a few of the names mentioned.

Al Sweeney, perhaps IMCA's most famous promoter (although now retired) — tells it this way.

"We've had so many great drivers run with us over the years . . . we were sort of a training ground for greatness. I'd have to say that Jan Opperman was one of the most thrilling of them all."

Not to be overlooked in this brief survey of Midwestern motorsport are the non-aligned, open competition racers . . . or outlaws, as they are usually tagged. Of all the Sprint racers, the outlaws may be the toughest customers of all. No restrictions or rules govern them . . . big motors, bigger tires . . . it's a "suck in your guts", "run what you brung" proposition. Lured by large pay-offs and the freedom of "do your own thing" racing, the outlaws roam anywhere they please.

A favorite stop is the historic half-mile at Knoxville, Iowa. Offering a lightning-quick turf comprised of black Iowa dirt, river-bottom muck and liberal doses of moisture-producing livestock manure — Knoxville draws some fast-moving characters each week. Also, late in the season a multi-day fiasco is held, called the Knoxville Sprint Car Nationals. It is a generally accepted fact that this spectacular happening has become America's most prestigious Sprint Car meet.

Like many drivers in the area, Jan Opperman — after he got established — campaigned both with IMCA and the outlaws. Fittingly, his greatest accomplishments were to come with the desperado contingent . . . in fact, he was and still is called "The King of the Outlaws".

But we are getting ahead of ourselves. Let Jan pick up the story, himself, and explain how all of this became reality.

"Living up to his promise, Yogi took Teacia and me right to Bill Smith's place in Lincoln, Nebraska. Smith was very nice but there was no ride available in any of his equipment. The season was well underway and he was already committed to other drivers. However, he did have a suggestion . . . Bill said we should call a friend of his, Bob Trostle[1], over in Des Moines, Iowa.

"Several things really startled me about the Midwest," Jan comments in retrospect. "Everything was so open and empty . . . a little bit like the Rocky Mountains if a great power had just rolled them out flat as a pool table. But it was the people that best caught my attention. They were totally different from Northern Californians . . . I must have appeared mighty strange to them, yet they were so kind and anxious to help. After meeting a few Midwesterners, I understood how Mary Lou came to be the way she was. Before going to California, she had just been a farm-country girl.

"One thing for sure, I didn't waste much time following Bill Smith's advice," Jan adds. "Wanting to get something started, I called Trostle's place in Des Moines. When he came to the phone, I introduced myself and got the surprise of my life. 'Yeah, I've heard of you,' he said. 'You're the guy I read about in the racing papers, who gave the California Offies a run for their money with an old V8-60.'

"It is impossible to describe my feelings at that moment. This guy, clear back in Iowa, had heard of me . . . he'd read about me in the racing papers. Let's face it, I was barely aware that racing papers existed — let alone that I'd been mentioned in them." (Even now, ten years later, Jan seems amazed by Trostle's recognition of him.)

"When I recovered from the shock, I questioned Mr. Trostle about a possible driving opportunity. He replied by saying that his only operable car was assigned to Earl Wagner[2]. Later on, I found out that Wagner sure knew what

[1] Bob Trostle has long been one of the great builders and team managers in all of Sprint Car racing. His designs are consistently excellent only to be exceeded by the workmanship found in the finished product.

[2] In the opinion of this author, Wagner rates as one of the hardest runners in my memory. He was never a true professional racer but worked full-time as a plumber around his home town of Pleasantville, Iowa. Concentrating solely on dirt-tracking Sprinters, he was known by those in the trade as a rim rider. Otherwise, he drove dangerously near the outer railings, using the cushion of loose dirt found there, to obtain greater speed. Currently he is retired from driving and serves as an official at Knoxville.

to do with his right foot — he was a gas-puncher; but at that time, upon hearing those words, my heart sunk. We were just ready to hang up, with me feeling a little sick, when Bob Trostle came up with an idea.

"You know," Jan remarks, pausing momentarily to reconstruct his memory, "I believe that I can quote him exactly . . . his offer was that important to me.

" 'Jan, there is another car,' " Mr. Trostle said. " 'It's nearly new . . . hardly been run at all. When I built it there were some changes I made that most drivers didn't like. Nobody wanted to drive it . . . so it has just been sitting in a barn ever since. The car is covered with hay and cobwebs, but IMCA runs the Iowa State Fairgrounds next weekend . . . if you want, I'll drag it out and you can give the thing a whirl.' "

Jan Opperman chuckles at the thought of his reaction to Trostle's suggestion. "He had scarcely finished what he was saying before I agreed to the deal. It's hard to play cool and professional when you're so desperate. A bit later, however, I began to wonder about my sanity. Hay . . . cobwebs . . . a car so weird that it had spooked these big-time racers. Oh boy, I thought to myself . . . you crazy kraut, you've really done it now.

"Bein' both hungry and true to my word, I headed for Des Moines . . . all the while thinkin' about this junky box that I was supposed to drive," Opperman confesses. "But when I got there and saw the car . . . I just couldn't believe my eyes. It was a beautiful race car . . . better than any I had seen in California. No, it wasn't fancy . . . not a lot of paint and chrome like California Sprinters. Trostle had spent his money on the very ultimate in necessary equipment. Midwesterners aren't into blowin' eyeballs apart with flashy machinery . . . they're just racers, interested in fast, effective cars.

"After I crawled into that fire breather, there at the Iowa Fairgrounds, I truly realized the quality of Bob Trostle's car. The thing was super . . . it really howled and slung dirt all over the place."

In keeping with the tradition of good story telling, it would be nice to report that Jan Opperman dazzled his IMCA rivals in the Iowa event. Nice . . . yes . . . but that was simply not the case. His performance was creditable, although not spectacular. The car — suffering from its long exile from the tracks — was a bit rusty mechanically and Jan, no doubt, had to be a little nervous.

Nevertheless, one week later at the Nebraska State Fair's half-mile clay oval, the dazzling did take place. With all traces of hay, cobwebs and nerves cast aside, Opperman decimated one of the finest fields of IMCA racers ever assembled. A car, supposedly unworthy of competition, teamed with a driver, who had long been haunted by the harsh judgments of others, won the prestigious race. After the checkered flag had signaled Jan's victory, plenty of head shaking took place. How could such a thing have happened? That peculiar car, an unknown driver — how could it have happened?

Characteristically in line with Jan's ever-present modesty, he explains it this way:

"Much of it had to do with the car," he says. The reason drivers were spooked by it was that Bob Trostle, genius that he is, had set the motor 2½ inches back of center. Those guys were great chauffeurs but they were used to setups where engines lay at center or ahead of center. Naturally, the car felt strange to them. Then I came along . . . I hadn't driven enough race cars to either know or care where the motor was in the chassis. I didn't need to get used to anything new . . . it was all new to me. Here's the important thing — today's dirt trackin' Sprinters all have their motors 5½ inches back of center.* Mr. Trostle and his car were just way ahead of the times and I blindly stumbled into a good deal."

Jan and Trostle won no more races in 1968, but a firm friendship was established. A friendship that prevails to the present day.

*Jan is making reference to the fact that current trends in dirt track racing call for motor locations far back of the car's center point. On the other hand, Sprinters running primarily on pavement have their engines mounted on center or ahead of center.

"I'll always love ol' Bob Trostle," Opperman remarks. "What a fabulous person . . . famous builder, big-shot racer . . . yet he's still only a plain ol' Iowa dude. He never tries to put you down or pull some of that classy stuff with anyone . . . I really care for him."

At the conclusion of the 1968 season Jan knew where his destiny lay, at least for the time being. Midwestern dirt tracks and the spine-chilling Sprint Cars, that gleefully ripped apart clay turf from North Dakota to Texas, had collectively flashed him the brightest green light of his life.

"The '68 season had hardly ended before I began thinking about 1969. I had always believed I could drive race cars; now there were some other people who agreed with me."

Jan Opperman

Butch Had Never Seen People Like Us Before

1969 proved to be a smashing success for Opperman's racing endeavors. He signed on with Bill Smith and became the regular pilot of the fast-moving Speedway Motors Sprinter. Their efforts were aimed at both IMCA and the brutal Outlaw action . . . chiefly the Outlaw action at Eagle Speedway (Lincoln) and Knoxville, Iowa.

"That's the big reason I went with Smith," Jan elaborates. "He had been impressed with my driving at The Nebraska State Fair, the previous year, and he suggested that I join up with him in 1969. He also said expenses were no object; that he intended to enter every race possible — IMCA or otherwise. That suited me fine . . . I needed the experience and definitely needed the money.

"We did well . . . in fact, Smith and I have always done well . . . together we've won a bundle of races. Back then I thought I was in 'fat city' . . . three hundred or four hundred dollars a week — above my expenses. Whewie — to a guy who had been livin' on nickels and dimes . . . all that money was unbelievable. Gettin' paid for doing something that I would have gladly done for nothing, or maybe even have paid for the privilege of doing — just unbelievable."

Jan stopped momentarily, pondering his present day financial problems. "Praise the Lord, but I could go for that amount of bucks right now. What the heck, I'm poor again, but I'm a happier man today," he noted.

Bill Smith — a man with over thirty years of accumulated racing experience — has a veritable wealth of Opperman memories at his access. Some of them were shared with me in the preparation of this chapter and are now quoted.

"When Steve (Yogi) first called me from California about Jan, I was laid up in the hospital and in pretty bad shape. An errant race car wheel had broken my leg, a blood clot had formed in my lung . . . racing was the last thing on my mind. Anyway, Yogi said they would be coming back to Nebraska almost immediately.

"At the time they arrived in Lincoln I was still hurting. I tried to be nice but you know how it is when you're sick. On the day the Nebraska State Fair Race was held, I attended it in a wheel chair. Watching Opperman drive was an amazing experience . . . what a God-given talent. He was so good . . . he didn't even seem to be aware of how good he was.

"In the weeks that followed, we made plans to team up for the 1969 season. I ordered a new Roger Beck-built Sprinter for him but it wasn't ready in time, so we began things with an old IMCA relic . . . a couple of Jan's friends did the mechanical work. Eventually, the new car arrived and business really picked up.

"Although Jan had some difficulty at Knoxville, he was a natural at Eagle Speedway. My old driver, Lloyd Beckman, was king there and did they ever wage some battles. Great duels . . . just great duels. One would win one week and the other the next. We also picked up three IMCA victories that year.

"If Jan Opperman had any fault as a driver it was that he was so darned aggressive. Never content to be a follower, he would invariably try to seize the lead on the first turn of the first lap . . . usually with a full-bore outside passing tactic. That's a risky move and we had some crunched machinery to prove it. Even now, I have a stack of busted wheels in my basement, left over from those days.

"But the record stands, Jan Opperman has owned one of the greatest God-given talents I've ever seen — or hope to see — for driving race cars. Like a great artist or a great anything — the talent was there. Even with so little experience behind him, the man was head and shoulders above most of his rivals."

"Yeah, I'll agree with Bill . . . to a point," Jan replies in response to Smith's observation. "It's hard for a young driver to figure out how, when and where to pass people . . . you can't always smoke 'em. Occasionally the time comes to 'out-finesse' the other guys . . . sort of sneak by 'em. On the other hand, nobody wins Sprint Car races by being conservative. From green flag to checker it is basically a 'foot to the floor trip'. Take charge, psych out the other drivers — push your car to the brink of crashing in the turns.

"As for outside passes you'll have to figure out just which dudes will accept that kind of move. Some hairy characters can't control their own cars too well and slide into you . . . then it's the wall or over the wall," Opperman nods painfully. "Others — and I hate to say this — will purposely slide-job* the high runner."

Outlaw half miles, slide-jobs, and mangled racing wheels — each of these, as of 1969, had become a major part of Jan Opperman's life within the dirt tracking community. Not unlike one of the twisting thunderstorms so prevalent during summer nights on the prairie, Jan rumbled over the dark earth to motorsport fame. All of the racing papers were writing about him then and the headlines, currently reposing in scrapbooks, are living proof to his accelerated broadslide to glory. "OPPERMAN FAST-RISING MIDWESTERN

*A slide-job is a particularly sinister tactic employed in dirt track racing. When an unscrupulous driver, running on the inside of a track, feels he is about to be passed on the outside — he will allow his machine to drift up into the other's path. The outside-traveling driver, providing he has time, has to back off. In all fairness, the move is usually intended as a bluff, but too often accidents have resulted — with the outside driver generally getting the worst of things.

STAR", "EAGLE SPRINT FIELD FALLS TO OPPERMAN", "RACING HIPPIE CLAIMS TOPEKA LOOT" . . . week after week, the typewriter keys clicked out their messages.

On the other hand, talking with Opperman at the present time, one quickly realizes that his fondest recollections of the summer of '69 have little to do with Sprint Cars or "fat city" wages. Jan had just purchased a new home for his family — a small farm near the town of Beaver Crossing, Nebraska (thirty-five miles west of Lincoln). He and Mary Lou were together and they had a new baby daughter (Krystal), born the previous year. Things were looking up for the Oppermans . . . in fact, an entirely different way of life lay just around the corner.

"Heck, it wasn't much of a farm," Jan relates, "but it was our first real home . . . the first place where we truly felt a sense of belonging.

"Let me confess something," he continues. "I had become a first class paranoid individual when it came to straight people. Paranoia is not of God, but I was yet to learn that. Except for racing contacts, my only associations were with hippies. Straights . . . man, they were bad news and were to be avoided at all costs. If a straight guy came to my house I would pretend to be away and not answer the door. Things had become so bad that I had my whole family going the same route, lying on the floor in silence when a non-hippie approached our home. Wow, what a paranoiac I was.

"The day after moving into the Beaver Crossing place, I got caught, however. Working at some project in the yard, I didn't notice this guy come strolling up, until too late. There was no way to duck him . . . no time to hide. And was he ever straight . . . a butch haircut, just a regular red neck type. Uh — oh — I thought to myself — now you crummy hippie, you're goin' to hear all about it.

"Well, this crewcut gent (he was just about my age) walked right up to me and stuck out his hand. Said his name was Butch Schernikau and that he owned a farm down the road.

'You folks need anything,' he told me, 'come over and help yourself. Use my tools or the tractor, my freezer is full of fresh-killed beef — take anything that you need.'

"I didn't know what to say," Jan admits, "a man that I had wanted to hide from was offering to share his most important possessions. Most likely he thought us to be poor and in need of help. We weren't, but God knows we looked it . . . shaggy hair, old clothes, beat-up station wagon. No doubt, Butch had never seen people like us before . . . hippies were a little scarce around Beaver Crossing.

"How about this guy? He knew nothing about us . . . we looked weird as hell to him . . . yet, all he wanted to do was help. His eyes, I'll never forget those eyes . . . so filled with warmth. His lamps were really lit. What a difference from California, where most of my acquaintances were takers not givers. Out there, if such an offer had been made, some dude would have showed up with a semi-truck and loaded all of Butch's belongings on board.

"That night," Jan proclaims, "I made up my mind to visit Butch the next day. 'Far out', I told Mary, 'this person would make a great hippie . . . all he needs is a little grass to smoke and some long hair.' I was still thinking dope was pretty important . . . not the world's salvation . . . but pretty important.

"It was drizzling the following morning when I slogged on over to Butch's place," Opperman recalls. "Clutchin' a bag of my best "pot", I found him knee-deep in sloppy cow manure, shoveling it into a spreader. Well, wearing my boots — I just walked out into the goop and began my speech. I talked about my trip . . . the crazy spiritualism, marijuana and the merits of being a hippie.

"Understand this," Jan remarks in contemporary explanation, "I thought I was doing him a favor. He was willing to share the best he had with me and I was only tryin' to do the same for him.

"Anyway, ol' Butch never said a word; he just kept on shoveling and listening to my deal. Only when I was finished, did he put down his shovel and make a comment. He laid no judgments on me . . . never once told me how screwed up I was . . . but the message was heavy nonetheless. I carry those words with me, right to this moment.

" 'Jan,' Butch said, 'one of us is wrong . . . we can't both be right. Christianity is my thing — Jesus answers my problems. Having the strength of Christ behind me, I don't need anything else. If you're ever interested, I'll be glad to help you start ridin' with the Lord.'

"All the way home, I thought about what Butch had told me. He hadn't been pushy like some other Christians I'd known . . . not critical or superior acting. Besides, he was so happy, so full of love . . . he was obviously doin' better with life than I. This guy really had somethin' going for himself and trudgin' along in the rain I decided to give Butch's program a try. I'd tried everything else . . . what did I have to lose? That was easily the greatest day of my life."

1969 . . . the year when Jan Opperman began to win the big races. It was also the year that he traded in the badge of Satan for the cross of Jesus. He has been wearing it ever since.

Jan ready for a flat-track race. (Opperman collection)

Right: A white sportcoat, bow tie and a carnation, Opperman was a clean-cut lad for high school graduation. (Opperman collection)

Below: The result of a flat-track race, Jan wound up with a broken ankle here. (Opperman Collection)

Conference at Indy: Jan talks about his car's gauges with owner Parnelli Jones, left, assistant Jimmy Dilamarter, right and chief mechanic Johnny Capels. (Chini)

Jan duels with a young Jimmy Caruthers (outside) during his formative years in Midget competition. The site was California's Ascot Speedway. (Chini)

Above: Jan referred to this mount as the "hay and cobweb" car which opened the door to Midwestern racing for him. Scene is Hutchinson, Kansas. (Byers)

Right: Bob Trostle, the car builder who gave Jan his first Midwestern ride. Trostle is one of the nation's most respected Sprint car builders. Photo taken in 1977 when Sprint star Doug Wolfgang was driving for him. (Dr. Hunter)

Below: Jan spins in front of Dave Ross at Hutchinson. Opperman is wiping the mud from his face. (Byers)

Jan made his Eastern debut memorable in Harold Hank's Sprint car. The car was constructed by noted California builder Don Edmunds and hadn't previously been successful. (Stamm)

Bill Smith, proprietor of one of the largest mail-order speed shops in the United States recognized Opperman's talent, and installed him in one of his Speedway Motors Sprinters. The team was very successful. Photo taken at Eagle Speedway in Lincoln. (Byers)

Opperman shares a victory lane celebration with his mechanic John Singer, bearded, and car owner Bill Smith, right, after a win at the IMCA Winternationals in 1974.

Jan's family, minus Teacia: From left, Krystal, young Jan (better known as Brother Boy) wife Mary Lou and daughter Jay Lou. (Clum)

Jan's most impressive competition on the Eastern circuit always came from talented Kenny Weld, who's shown here with his father, "Pappy".

Covered with mud and sporting a bloody nose from a wheel-thrown rock, Jan has just defeated the USAC Sprint field at Eldora Speedway. March 31, 1974.

Jan has always spoken highly of one Mitch Smith, an Eastern leadfoot who seemingly threw caution to the wind when he drove.

In his prime as an Outlaw, Opperman's gang visited the prestigious Hulman Classic in 1974 and nearly won the event. He's shown here on a time trial run. (Mahoney)

Above: Jan battles Pancho Carter at Reading in March, 1974. Opperman is in Dick Bogar's Car, no longer wearing its usual #99 (Mahoney) Below: The way to win on dirt. Speedway Motors Sprinter and Jan in a full-lock broad-slide at Terre Haute, Indiana's famed "Action Track." (Mahoney)

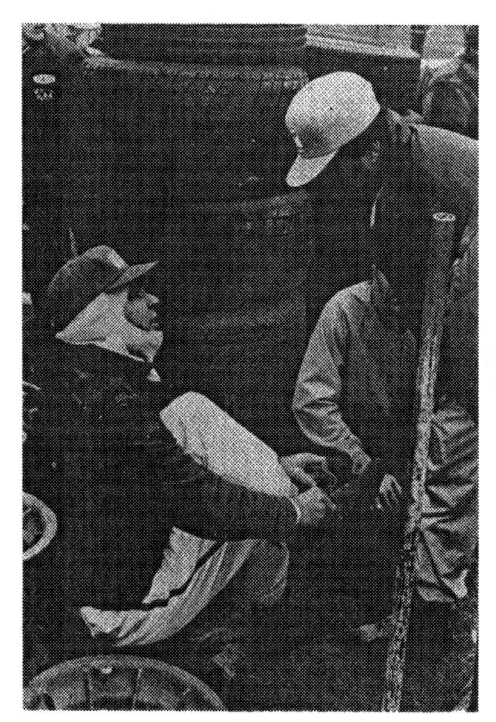

Above left: Race track friends: Jan is shown hugging pal Bubby Jones after Bubby drove Opperman's regular ride to an Eldora win in 1977. (Mahoney) Above right: A. J. Foyt takes a moment to talk with Jan prior to the start of a race. (Mahoney) Below: Three Sprint car stand-outs: Pennsylvania's Steve Smith (left) and Bobby Allen, who's an ace builder as well, rap with Opperman at Atlanta in 1977. (Marderness)

Opperman became fast friends with second generation driver James McElreath. Here, they're shown evaluating the dirt at Eldora in 1976. James was killed the following year in a Sprint crash. (*Mahoney*)

Below: This notice is not in the cockpit of Opperman's car, but illustrates the attitude necessary to successfully drive a Sprint car. (*Sharp*)

When Opperman arrived at Indianapolis, he was shaggy and looked liked a product of the road. Note he's borrowed a jacket from fellow racer Tom Bigelow. (*Chini*)

Below: Parnelli Jones said, "Anyone who's put their head on the chopping block 85-90 times per year in a Sprint car has to have something going for him," and he gave Opperman a ride at Indy. (*Mahoney*)

Here Jan is shown removing the traditional three rookie stripes from his Speedway car upon successful completion of his test. (Mahoney)

Right: Amiable Sammy Sessions befriended Opperman at the Indianapolis Motor Speedway. Sessions was himself a Sprint car champ and later lost his life in a snowmobile accident. (Mahoney)

Below: The Viceroy Special that made Opperman a starter in the 1974 Indianapolis 500.

Above: Jan is shown qualifying for for the ill-fated 1976 Hoosier Hundred. (Mahoney)

Left: After the Hoosier Hundred, announcer Sid Collins joined with Bubby Jones and June Cochran in offering a prayer for Jan. (Mahoney)

Right: Crash sequence at the 1976 Hoosier Hundred: Opperman chases Parsons, Parsons spins, Opperman (12) thunders into the stalled vehicle and is followed by pal Bubby Jones. Later, Chuck Gurney slammed into the melee and Opperman received serious head injuries. (Crist & Mahoney)

Left: Jan was extremely popular with members of the press at Indy. (Chini)

Below: The Routh Meat Packing Special that Jan ran in the 1976 race.

JAN OPPERMAN'S TOP IMCA FINISHES FOR 1969

Date	Location	Finish	Car
June 8	Des Moines (Iowa State Fairgrounds)	First Place	Speedway Motors Special
Aug. 17	Des Moines (Iowa State Fairgrounds)	Second Place	Speedway Motors Special
Aug. 23	Des Moines (Iowa State Fairgrounds)	First Place	Speedway Motors Special
Aug. 24	Sedalia, Missouri (Mile Track)	Fifth Place	Speedway Motors Special
Sept. 6	Topeka, Kansas (Mid-America Fair)	First Place	Speedway Motors Special
Sept. 7	Topeka, Kansas (Mid-America Fair)	Third Place	Speedway Motors Special
Sept. 12	Spencer, Iowa (Clay County Fair)	Second Place	Speedway Motors Special

*1,105 total points for seventh place in the IMCA final standings.

"The Groves"

The epitome of cultural conflict . . . that's what Southeastern Pennsylvania is. The lush, green hills bordering the Susquehanna River fortify the last stand for Nineteenth Century American living. The same goes for the flat, fertile farmlands off toward Lancaster. Although frequently referred to as Pennsylvania Dutch Country, that title is, in itself, a misnomer. The people whose culture has dominated the region for generations are of German descent . . . many of them still clinging to the rigid customs of the Amish religious sects.

And so the draft horses, lathered with sweat, tug the heavy farm implements; threshing machines separate the grain and narrow, winding roads connect the off-beat, sleepy villages. Barn raisings, hex signs and covered bridges . . . when in the area one expects to find William Jennings Bryan giving a speech in support of the free and unlimited coinage of silver. Somewhere, just over the next hill, John Deere is probably demonstrating his first steel plow. Southeastern Pennsylvania is that sort of place — a downright excursion into the time machine's magical wanderings.

Still, not everyone residing along the Susquehanna is a proponent of horsedrawn vehicles and that's where the cultural conflict comes in. For that same corner of the Keystone State is also a bastion of dirt track automobile racing . . . namely the variety of motorsport exemplified by the savage thrusts of Sprint cars. Cultural conflict . . . I should say. Where else could you view a pickup truck, towing a trailered Sprinter over a mere sliver of rural asphalt, struggling to pass a prancing Amishman's trotter and black-lacquered buggy?

Sprint Car competition, in those parts, is about as old as the above-mentioned green hills. Nobody remembers when the tradition actually began but its support has often approached the frenzy of religious fanaticism. "Larger than life" heroes emerged from all this piston-driven enthusiasm . . . men like Tommy Hinnershitz,* who still speaks with a thick German accent and drove Sprints as if tomorrow had no chance of appearing.

All of the ancient popularity notwithstanding, the real zenith in Pennsylvania Sprint Car racing prestige began in the late Sixties and continued for several years. Although several tracks were involved, two provided the key to the movement's success . . . the spectacular dirt half-miles at Williams Grove and Selinsgrove. "The Groves", as they are affectionately referred to by the thousands who patronize them, had long known national fame but — during the years of discussion — they would become the stages for some of the grandest Sprint Car clashes for all time.

The leadership in this open-cockpit epoch was a brilliant promoter and clever public relations specialist, Jack Gunn who died of cancer in 1980. A one-time track announcer at Williams Grove, who had evolved into the position of operator of the speedway, Gunn's idea was to make the area a mecca for dirt-tracking outlaws. With Williams Grove's tacky clay as the command post and Selinsgrove as a team facility — Jack

*Tommy (pronounced Tummy by local people) was perhaps the greatest dirt driver in Sprint Cars ever. Headquartered at his farm near Oley, Pennsylvania, he ventured forth weekly to win so many main events that even he lost count, long ago. Balding, paunchy and well past fifty — Hinnershitz was still defeating the best American dirt racers when severe arthritis in his hands forced retirement upon him in 1960. Seven times (1949, '50, '51, '52, '55, '56 and 1959), Tommy captured AAA and USAC Eastern Sprint Car Championships.

Gunn offered some of the largest weekly purses yet to be presented.

His hopes were not disappointed . . . the iron-gripped outlaw racers came from far and near. There were no rules, no engine limitations . . . no restrictions of any kind. From this open competition, "no-holds-barred" system — the wildest Sprint Cars to appear in anyone's imagination, developed. Monster motors set way behind center, huge wings or airfoils fastened atop their roll cages, weird and freaky tire combinations — these flame-flicking beasts were turned loose on the deep Pennsylvania turf.

The Tracks were prepared with loose surfaces (soft and mushy) to accommodate the fearsome power of their weekend travelers. The end result was a mud-slinging war, the intensity of which is almost impossible to describe with pencil and paper.

Onto this scene, in 1970, strolled Jan Opperman. Before moving on, several years later, Jan's popularity in the region had easily approached that of his lionized predecessor — the beloved Hinnershitz. The account of Opperman's coming to Pennsylvania touches on the incredible and is best told by Jack Gunn, the man responsible for its happening.

> "Naturally, I was always looking for talent to bring into our racing circuit . . . we wanted the best drivers around. In February of 1970 the IMCA Sprints were running, as usual, at the old Florida Fairgrounds in Tampa and a business associate of mine was there," Mr. Gunn remembers.
>
> "He called me up home and said, 'Jack, you'd better get down here . . . there's a guy here named Jan Opperman, who's the darndest racer I've ever seen. He's really something.'
>
> "Having nothing to do, I went on down to Tampa. At the next race we got there quite early and I asked my buddy to point Jan Opperman out. He did and I almost fell over . . . what a wild and woolly looking character. He had long scraggly hair and sported an old worn-out

cowboy hat and a purple and white driver's suit. The only hippies I'd ever seen were on television and I had no desire to get any closer to one — let alone take him to Pennsylvania. My mind was already made up — I wanted no part of this Opperman.

"When the racing finally started, I grudgingly had to admit that he was a super driver. Even with the old "box" he was in, the guy could sure fly. He was loaded with talent but I was still leery of him. I figured him for an outlaw in the purest sense of the word.

"After the race was over I was walking out the back gate, when I heard someone call my name. It was Opperman. He walked up, introduced himself and again I almost fell over. How deceiving . . . he was one of the nicest, most humble and polite men I'd ever met around a race track. Not only that but he was beautifully well spoken and had an uncanny way of expressing himself. At that time, he told me he was interested in racing in Pennsylvania — if he could get a ride. Jan gave me his address and phone number in Nebraska where he could be reached. Still in shock, I stumbled around verbally and said I'd see what I could do."

Jack Gunn continues:

"I watched the rest of the Tampa meet and became even more impressed with Jan's driving. He had a unique style . . . very different from most racers. Afterwards, on the way home to Pennsylvania, I got to thinking about Opperman. What a drawing card he would be — one way or the other . . . a real live hippie running at "The Groves".

"The big problem was finding him a ride in a good, local car. People around home are extremely conservative and it was hard to imagine many of them approving of Jan's mode of living. Plus, there are always more good drivers around Pennsylvania than cars.

"Nevertheless, as the season approached, I grew more enthused about the Opperman deal and started sniffing around for any available rides. There was nothing open.

"But then something happened that set the ball rolling. Harold Hank, one of the area's more dedicated owners, lost his driver in a Midget accident . . . he was seriously injured and would be out of action for some weeks to come. I got in touch with Hank and found him very discouraged . . . he was just going to park his Sprinter until the regular man was ready. 'I know of a guy who's one hell of a driver . . . he's from Nebraska and wants to race in this area', I told him. Harold wasn't interested, however.

"Perhaps I should explain a little about Harold Hank's situation. He owned a black Edmunds-built machine. It was beautiful and Harold spent plenty of money . . . yet, he had known limited success. No offense to Don Edmunds, but Sprinters of his construction have never done well in Pennsylvania. Harold may have loved that car . . . just the same he was ready to win some races.

"A short time later, Hank called me back. 'I've been thinking,' he said, 'if this man in Nebraska is as good as you say, I might try him — at least temporarily.'

"I phoned Jan immediately and told him a ride was available for the Selinsgrove and Williams Grove openers. He was excited and promised to hustle himself East as soon as possible.

"So Jan came, all the way from Nebraska, and he surely hadn't polished himself up any. His hair looked longer, faded Levis, flannel shirt and those fringed moccasins he always wore . . . I began to have doubts all over again. Let me tell you, Harold Hank was the most conservative individual in a very conservative society. But I built up my courage and drove Jan over to Hank's shop to get them acquainted with each other.

"Harold took one look at Opperman and nearly had a stroke. He got me aside and really put the words to me. 'Gunn,' he fumed, 'not only is that weirdo not goin' to drive my car — I don't even want him hangin' around my shop. Get him out of here — you know I don't have any truck with long-hairs and the like.' "

Jack Gunn laughs in retrospect, as he recalls his desperate attempts to placate the raging car owner.

"Trying to stay calm, I attempted to reason with Hank. 'You're not being fair,' I told him. 'Opperman has come clear from Nebraska . . . you're judging him solely by his looks and not by what he can do. Believe me, he's not as bad as he appears and he can really drive. Stick to your promise and give the guy a chance.'

"Harold thought a while and then he replied, 'O.K., I'm a man of my word, but that shaggy character had better be good.' "

That shaggy character was better than good. The season opened on a chilly Saturday night at Selinsgrove. Opperman — apparently unaware of the no-win reputation of Edmunds-built Sprinters in Pennsylvania — turned Hank's black number four inside out and came within a wheel turn of winning the feature. He finished second. The next afternoon at Williams Grove, Jan really got himself hooked-up. He slashed through the wheel-banging traffic to victory and thoroughly humiliated the best of Jack Gunn's dirt-tracking outlaws.

"It was an unprecedented thing," Gunn proclaims. "No driver had ever blown into Pennsylvania and smoked our people like that. And it has never happened since. Think about that . . . Jan had seen neither the tracks nor the car before and he was able to do so well. What a talent! Anyway, he sure got me off the hook with Harold Hank . . . Harold was thrilled. Jan was tied up in Nebraska and couldn't relocate his family at that time; so Harold paid for plane tickets to allow Opperman to commute, until other arrangements could be made."

"Winnin' that first race at Williams Grove is one of my great racing thrills . . . maybe the greatest," Jan Opperman adds. "I had wanted to come over there because — after talkin' to many people — that area seemed to offer the best quality of dirt racing on a steady basis. I've always figured that you're only as good as the competition you drive against . . . doing well in Pennsylvania would help establish me as a fast, classy racer. I knew that some Pennsylvania folks kind of frowned on me . . . after all, I wasn't too beautiful. But I wasn't there to enter a beauty contest . . . drivin' dirt cars was my thing. I proved I could do that."

Sadly, Jan's jubilation was short-lived. In June of 1970, Jay Opperman died. While making his Midwest Sprint Car debut at Knoxville, Iowa, young Jay's machine contacted another car and flew out of the track — killing him instantly.

"I was in Pennsylvania when the news reached me . . . it just about tore my head off," Jan recalls, his voice husky with emotion and tears welling up in his eyes. "It . . . it was the most awful feeling I've ever known.

"In a sense it was my fault. He hadn't been racin' much lately, 'cause California had been no better to him than to me. I called Jay and encouraged him to come to Beaver Crossing — keep his family at Mary's and my place — and go Sprint Car racin'. We had big plans . . . we were aiming to save our money, buy a place in the Rocky Mountains and go country — like when we were kids.

"I loved my brother so much and I ought to have known him better. He would never have been content to break in gradually . . . not Jay, he was a fire eater . . . a real hard-nosed dude. I should've been there with him — I never stopped to realize that his enormous raw ability was no match for a low experience level. Perhaps my guidance might have helped — I don't know.

"When I learned the details of the accident, I felt worse," Jan goes on, his voice beginning to crack. "He was really flyin' . . . sailin' high and wide. He had roared outside a very fast driver, when the other guy's torsion stop broke. This caused the inside car to lurch into my brother. Jay went end over end through the fence and flipped forever. He was so tough and brave . . . yet, when one of those things jumps on your head . . . well, Jay simply never had a chance. Trapped by his inexperience and great desire . . . it should've been another way.

"I went out there, buried him and faced his wife* and kids. Did a lot of cryin' too. The worst of it was, he would've been better than I. He was always better than I — just not as lucky. In 1977, when James McElreath was killed at Winchester, Indiana — it was as though Jay had died all over again. Except for bein' so quiet, James was very much like Jay had been. Anyway, I've got that ranch in the mountains, the way we had planned. I like to think Jay Opperman is up there in those woods — somewhere — 'cause it's sure where he loved to be."

As a sidelight to this tragic story, Jan Opperman, himself, returned to Knoxville, Iowa in August of 1971. On a series of humid nights, he won the prestigious Knoxville Sprint Car Nationals. Just as if to say that no race track, regardless of its toughness, could beat the Oppermans.

Judge not according to the appearance.

John 7:24

*Jay Opperman's widow, undaunted by the cruelties of auto racing, eventually married Jimmy Boyd — another daring outlaw racer.

"You Gotta Go On"

Despite being crushed by his brother's death, Jan went at the unruly Sprint Cars with increased intensity.

"Sure, I can wind up like Jay . . . busted all to pieces," Jan told me several months after the younger Opperman's crash. "But it's simply too late to turn back now . . . you gotta go on. If one of those fire-breathin' animals tears off both my arms tomorrow, I'll still praise God for lettin' me be a racer. Not only that . . . quittin' wouldn't bring back Jay."

Although Jan frequented the National Outlaw Circuit — his main efforts continued to be directed at Jack Gunn's dirt tracks and other speed facilities in that part of Pennsylvania. The increasing number of available weekly races — with their inflated purses — made Keystone State Sprint competition tough to resist. "You could race three or four times a week and hardly travel at all," he recalls. "At $700 and up to win each feature, it was a fat country to be in."

Thus it was that Opperman had decided to move his family to Pennsylvania — at least for the months offering auto racing. They rented a weathered old farmstead, high up among the stern hills, west of Selinsgrove. The nearest community was tiny Beaver Springs and their only neighbors were the stony-faced Amish, with black, buttonless clothes and silent-running buggies. These weren't the affluent Amish farmers — gawked at by tourists over in Lancaster County, but, instead, a hard-pressed mountain people who carved a living from hillside fields, using single-bottomed walking plows.

I well remember a warm, summer day when this writer attempted to visit Jan at his Appalachian retreat. The Oppermans were away so I parked myself down near the road to await their return. Before long, two Belgian horses, lugging a battered hay wagon and steered by an ancient Amishman, came into view. As the huge beasts pulled abreast of me, their driver shot a furtive glance at my car, nodded faintly in my direction and headed away at a slightly faster pace. Clip-clop — the vision soon disappeared around a curve and a strange thought occurred to me. Here — in this isolated spot — lived America's fastest dirt track racer; right smack in the middle of a group of folks whose only concern with horsepower had nothing to do with the internal combustion engine or any of its adaptations.

By 1972 Jan Opperman had dialed himself into a Sprint Car outfit, with whom he was to achieve everlasting renown — both in Pennsylvania and nationally. Led by car owner Dick Bogar and mechanic Ralph Heintzelman, and the backup Allen-built machine were both sponsored by Bogar's business — the Bogar Speed and Show Equipment shop of Beavertown, Pennsylvania.

No more unpretentious-looking race cars ever graced a dirt track. Painted orange and trimmed in black or midnight blue (I could never tell which), each of the brutish vehicles was usually well plastered with several weeks' collection of dried clay on their stone-chipped bodies and windshields. Beneath all the grime lurked the number ninety-nine . . . a numerical trademark that came to chill the hearts of many a brave soul.

As was the case with Opperman himself — the appearance of Bogar's Sprinters was deceiving. They were faster than the wind . . . particularly the Heintzelman creation. Of equal importance was their durability — they ran and ran, crashed and ran again. Presented as proof of this fact are the following statistics:

In 1972 Jan Opperman drove a Bogar Special in ninety-five Sprint Car races, an almost unheard of feat. He won fifty-two heats and forty-four main events. Added to this were:

12 second place main event finishes.
10 third place main event finishes.
7 fourth place main event finishes.
6 fifth place main event finishes.

In case your math is bad this means that Opperman and crew put together seventy-nine top five finishes in one slam-bang Sprint Car season . . . a mark that remains universally acclaimed by all knowledgeable members of the various open-cockpit clans. It may be an unbreakable record as few men or machines are as strong as Jan Opperman and "old 99".

"Yeah, that old orange box . . . we washed her about once a year, need it or not," Jan laughs. "Yup, sure did love that old car . . . just plain loved it. Probably '99' was the best Sprinter I ever drove, but the funny thing is the Bobby Allen-built second car was almost as good. Either one would flat-out run, they were both easy to set up . . . real adjustable pieces of equipment.

And that Ralph Heintzelman . . . let me tell you about him. Always chewin' on that tobacco of his . . . he'd shorten the frame, straighten the frame . . . build anything you needed. Like this old bum that drove her — that car may not have looked too pretty, but she was always ready to race. Why — 'cause Ralph had his stuff together. Another thing, that doggone Kraut (I can call him a Kraut, since I'm one too) knew those Pennsylvania tracks. They were tricky — real fast, tacky and dangerous — and he could usually guide me to the fast grooves and away from the holes."

"How about that '72 record for wins and finishes — is that one of your favorite accomplishments?" I once asked him.

"Records — this may sound phony — but I never think much about records," he replied. "We dragged around to as many races as we could get to and things worked out. It was our year. Still, in 1973 we had the same combination and there were plenty of problems . . . breakdowns, crashes and bad luck. Luck is a big factor in racing success — don't let anyone kid you. We won a bunch of features in '73 but never approached the previous year's achievement."

It would be impossible to discuss Opperman's exploits in Pennsylvania (and elsewhere) without mentioning Kenny Weld and the often-times bitter rivalry that blazed between these two spectacular drivers. Whereas the Weld-Opperman "tug of war" was a boon to fans, journalists and promoters, the situation worried inside members of both camps. Amidst the roar of the turf-ripping Sprinters there was a quiet deadliness about the whole thing . . . an anxious awaiting of the great crash that would end it all. On the positive side, the struggle between Jan and Kenny gave forth some of the most flamboyant displays of dirt track artistry yet seen between our widespread coasts.

Kenny Weld was younger in years than Opperman, but older in Pennsylvania racing experience. Coming from a distinquished motorsport family, he had left his Kansas City home to settle in York, Pennsylvania and was already well established within the area's Sprint Car fraternity when Jan drifted into the picture.

Thick in the waist — Kenny wore Amish-style glasses, had a thin, pointed nose and his forearms looked to have been transplants from a deceased village blacksmith. He was powerful and he was smart . . . extremely smart when it came to clay tracks and the cars that raced them. Most drivers have always turned up their noses at the greasy, mechanical jobs associated with racing. Not Kenny — even in his heyday as a Sprint Car pilot, he remained a very active mechanic.

Weld's greatest problem was his personality. Introverted and aloof, he made little effort to win friends with certain groups of fans and most journalists. Apparently, and rightfully so, he felt his driving skills sufficiently well developed to speak for him. He might have pulled it off but along came Opperman. Jan, being more than a good driver, was a born public-relations man. Warm and friendly, "Opp" talked to all people and continually had good words for and about everyone. Immediately, Weld found himself cast in the role of the ogre . . . especially by the younger fans who were fascinated by Opperman's long hair and frank conversation. Jan had his critics, of course, but they were far less vocal than the bleacher-dwelling youths who taunted Kenny Weld.

Subsequently, Weld — who seldom said anything — apparently began to talk. Never to me . . . I can recall no derogatory statements by Weld, about Opperman. But then Kenny seldom spoke to me in great detail on any matter. Whatever . . . fact or fiction — Weld quotes pertaining to Jan's hippie habits, long hair, dope, phony religious beliefs and dirty driving began to appear in the trade publications. Undoubtedly there was bad blood and the writers — always searching for a story — helped push hot temperatures past the boiling point. What great copy, if you care for that sort of thing . . . the redneck versus the hippie, conservative America locked in mortal combat with "the new left".

The mortal combat business was no joke — true combat prevailed in the dark turns at Williams Grove, on the long straightaways at Selinsgrove, and at other equally dangerous places along the outlaw trail. Plainly, the Opperman-Weld fandango had evolved into more than words, innuendos and yellow journalism.

Ken Weld was employed by Pennsylvania's most affluent and enthusiastic car owner, Bob Weikert. Mr. Weikert — a cattle buyer by trade — loved Sprint Car racing and was passionately fond of his fleet of immaculate red, white and blue machines. It should be said that Weikert, as of 1978, was consumed by the sport and owned six Sprinters which were utilized by Paul Pitzer — a one-time Weld protege.

Money has never been an object with Weikert. He frequently packs a roll of bills large enough to choke one of his "hamburgers on the hoof" to death and (past or present) he has been quick to spend any amount necessary to put a winner on the track. One of those gleaming Floyd Trevis[1] — built Sprint Cars, presently parked in his shop, has a strong reputation for doing some heavy winning. Nick-named "old Blue", the car was a particular favorite of Weld's and helped Kenny claim five consecutive Williams Grove Championships (1970-1974). Reportedly, "Old Blue" has been victorious in one hundred feature races . . . most of them being registered during the years when Kenny Weld was behind the wheel.

Weld and Weikert approached Sprint Car racing with a staunch dedication and they were extremely proud of their top-drawer operation. As an expression of that pride, they had a large supply of T-shirts silk-screened with the following message:

WELD — WEIKERT RACING
WHEN THE GREEN FLAG DROPS,
THE BULL !**! STOPS

Prophetic words, indeed . . . around the race track there was no bull about either Bob Weikert or Kenny Weld.

Accordingly, the battle lines were drawn and they went a lot deeper than a long-haired hippie, in a cowboy hat, jabbing at the establishment.

It was "low-budget" racing versus the "big bucks" variety, Bogar against Weikert and the "orange boxes" dueling with "Old Blue" and a brigade of snappy reinforcements. Who won? On the track it was most likely a fifty-fifty deal. In the overall tabulation, one finds a different result. Weikert's Livestock Specials still run "The Groves" but Dick Bogar is long gone from the game.[2] That fact speaks for itself.

While making the tapes and laying the foundation for our book, Jan and I discussed the hassle with Kenny Weld. "We

[1] Floyd Trevis, a brilliantly innovative but expensive builder, from Youngstown, Ohio has continually supplied Weikert with first-rate cars. I remember a long ago day when I asked Weld about the builder's identity of a particular Weikert Sprinter he was driving. Before answering, Ken glared at me in disbelief. "Trevis — who the hell do you think?" he finally snapped.

[2] Bogar may be gone but "Old 99" (the Heintzelman car) still runs. Wearing number five now, it is owned and driven by Larry Switzer at Port Royal (Pennsylvania) Speedway.

don't want to exploit that controversy; there was enough exploitation when it was happening," I noted.

"Right, there was plenty of that," Jan nodded in agreement. "Yet controversy did exist and there was a sure 'nuff feud . . . I guess. But that was never my trip, it was his and I want that in print.

"Kenny hated me so much . . . I don't think he does now . . . he did then, however. Understanding that is essential to understanding my success in Pennsylvania and elsewhere," Jan explained. Hatred leads to anger . . . anger and temper tantrums have no place in race cars or anything, for that matter. You lose your temper and you'll be a loser — all the way — for sure.

"Once the feud got going and Kenny's bad temper became so obvious — God forgive me — I used it to my advantage. I remember when I was just a little kid, Dad taught me . . . 'Jan, fightin' a real tough guy (tougher than you) — spit right in his face first. Hawk one smack in his eye ad you'll have him. He'll be roaring mad and nobody — no matter how good he is — can fight when he's mad.'

"I never forgot that," and "Oppie" grins a little. "It sure did work with Kenny. Oh I never spit in his face . . . not literally. On slow parade laps I'd pop him a bit in his back bumper or come up beside his car and rub nerf bars. Sometimes we'd meet in the pits and I'd say, 'Hey Kenny, I really love ya, you old redneck.' He'd start fumin' and carryin' on and the next thing he would drive too hard . . . kiss a wall or grind up his tires . . . somethin' foolish like that. The result was that I would beat him a few times, then he'd proceed to give me some races . . . all because of that darned temper. Kenny's temper and weird drivin' went hand in hand.

"You know," Jan says in earnest, "I really admired him and that's the pure truth. Except for his temper . . . I can never admire that. Still Kenny was such a professional, a complete student of racing . . . he had it all. In his head was so much knowledge and with his wits about him, Kenny's driving was superb. I ached for him then and ache for him right now.

You've heard about 'bein' your own worst enemy' . . . well, that was Kenny Weld — he didn't need any other enemies."

"Was Weld the fiercest driver in Pennsylvania when you were there?" I asked Jan in that same conversation.

"No — in all honesty — he wasn't," came the reply. "Kenny was a professional racer and even with all of Weikert's money behind him, he had to avoid crashes and finish races to earn a living.

"Mitch Smith* was the fiercest. He didn't make his living at it, but raced for fun . . . for the straight thrill of winning. Ol' Mitch . . . he'd go just as hard and heavy as necessary. Sometimes I thought that he was flat willing to die . . . just to win. Following him around really educated me and when I began to beat him a few times, I knew I was gainin' some class. Yup, Mitch Smith was the fiercest of them all and the Pennsylvania dudes were the toughest dirt racers in America."

Summing up the great Pennsylvania Sprint Car conflict and Jan Opperman's tour of duty at "The Groves" is a task best assigned to Jack Gunn. No man knows the situation better than he.

"From a promoter's point of view, the rivalry between Jan and Kenny was a gold mine . . . it really packed the people in our stands. But as a friend of each of them it worried the hell out of me. The thing was dynamite, particularly for Weld because he was always so up-tight.

"Ken was just that kind of person . . . terribly sensitive, easily depressed and addicted to winning. He was a dedicated, beautiful racer to watch — loaded with both race track and race car know-how. Nevertheless, possessing all that talent and armed with Bob's (Weikert) super equipment, Ken was no match for Opperman psychologically.

"Jan is right," Gunn contends, "he never started anything.

*Mitch Smith seldom backs off the throttle when racing. In 1971 — running on a temporary permit — he slaughtered USAC's Sprint stars on three consecutive Pennsylvania outings (twice at Williams Grove and once at Selinsgrove). Specializing in frightful flips, Smith prefers to drive Sprint Cars near his home at Linglestown, Pennsylvania; thus, many dirt-track fans have never seen this colorful driver perform.

He didn't have to. "Opp" could irritate Kenny by doing nothing. Just a smile, the crowds of people around him, his aggressive driving . . . all of these things tormented Kenny. Was Weld really offended by Jan's life-style, did he hate the hippie business, or were those just excuses to cover Ken's frustration? I have no way of knowing the answer and after all, I had wrongly judged Jan, myself, back in 1970 at Tampa.

"As for Jan, I count him as one of my best friends ever and that includes his entire family. All those raps hung on Jan . . . dirty hippie, dope, long hair . . . so much for them. In my relationship with him, he was always the perfect gentleman and never did I hear him bad-mouth anyone — not even Kenny.

"Because of my friendship with Opperman, there were those who accused me of giving him special deals, extra money and so forth. Let this stand for the record . . . anything Jan ever got from me, he earned three times over. Everyone benefited from the publicity he brought us and helped to create with both his fine attitude and heavy foot. There have been many excellent drivers on our circuit, Jan included, but unquestionably Opperman was the greatest personality.

"Considering his horrible accident in 1976, if Jan Opperman never races successfully again, he will forever be a beloved hero in this part of the country," Jack Gunn concludes.

Maybe so, but time marches on and yesterday's heroes go along with it — even at Williams Grove.

Yellow Breeches Creek still flows near the track's main gate and the zany, winged, flame-spitting monsters broadslide the shadowy turns each Friday night. But only a memory are those helmeted duelists of another time . . . the hippie and the redneck . . . Jan Opperman and Kenny Weld.

For reasons known chiefly to himself, Weld has retired from driving and currently runs a machine shop business in Kansas City.

Opperman, on the other hand, moved to USAC, Indianapolis and that brain-scrambling accident. Today, Jan once again squints through clay-smeared goggles, practicing one of his favorite axioms . . . "You Gotta Go On". And, no doubt, there are those moments when "Opp" — temporarily befuddled by blasting mud and thundering engines — hurriedly glances at his dirt-splashed foes and unconsciously wonders . . . Where's Kenny . . . I know he's runnin' somewhere close by.

He that is slow to anger is better than the mighty; and he that ruleth his spirit than he that taketh the city.
Proverbs 16:32

Never Call Me A Jesus Freak

Few things provoke Jan Opperman these days; he has learned to roll with the punches and accept God's will. But there are a couple of terms — often associated with him — which thoroughly test his patience.

First of all, don't refer to Jan's Christian trip as being a religion. "No, don't hook me up with religions; just say I'm a Christian," he requests. "The word religion implies a religious organization and that is exactly what I'm tryin' to escape. All men are my brothers . . . not just the members of a specific church. When I think about religion, I think of a whole bunch of righteous people, gathered around, laying heavy judgments on the supposedly unrighteous. Nobody should judge . . . Jesus didn't. He talked about love and understanding — not judging. To be a true Christian . . . you only have to accept Christ and the things he asks of us. There are no deals, no business propositions . . . and no social standing connected with that.

"The church part is O.K.; we have a little log church, up in Montana, that we built. But it's only a building and a simple one, indeed. No fancy place — just a warm, dry shelter where folks can make contact with The Lord, in comfort. The important thing is . . . churches are only buildings — nothing more. Jesus didn't require a church . . . he preached in the mountains, at the seashore . . . anywhere.

"I know that many people are into organized religions, attend huge, beautiful churches and firmly believe in what they're doing. Fine . . . who am I to knock their thing? Every man finds his own way . . . but don't tie me in with religion. That's not my operation."

Secondly, Jan Opperman doesn't care for the expression, "Jesus Freak". "Never call me a 'Jesus Freak'," and Jan isn't requesting with this statement. "I don't like to see the word freak connected with Jesus. Also, I'm no freak. If a label must be used for me . . . then let it be Jesus Man. I'm proud of my acceptance of Christ and certainly his teachings are no fad with me. For ten years I've been working to make myself a Christian and that length of time indicates no fad . . . it's serious business with this ol' bald-headed outlaw. The 'Jesus Freak' business . . . that was just another fad, like the hippie deal turned out to be."

As was described earlier, Opperman knew little about Christianity or the Bible until his meeting with Butch Schernikau in that Nebraska cow barn. There was no talk of Christian principles around his childhood homes. "I don't even know what faith we were supposed to practice," Jan observes.

Later on, like most hippies, he flirted with Christianity . . . hovering near its borders — sometimes crossing over and upon other occasions drifting far away.

"There was a lot of the Christian philosophy within our hippie beliefs — there was a lot of other stuff (way-out stuff) too," Opperman explains. "But mostly I was into spiritualism . . . communicatin' with spirits, prayin' to spirits and all that sort of thing. Also, I tried some of those Oriental cults that used to be so big in California . . . maybe they still are.

"Brother," he continues, "I even joined this church . . . they called it the Golden Gate Church. Supposedly it was a Christian experience but I learned otherwise, a few years later. Like many so-called Christians . . . they didn't give much thought to what Jesus had said. Anyway, I saw some mighty strange things happen in that place . . . situations so strange that nobody would believe me, even if I felt like describin' them.

"The most important thing is that before meeting Butch in 1969, and trying his idea, none of these other programs worked for me. I always felt hassled, pressured . . . continually mad at something or somebody. The only thing that could positively settle me down was dope . . . smokin' a big joint or whatever. No wonder I began to believe drugs were so all-fired essential."

"Come on, you weren't all that bad," chimes in Mary Lou Opperman. "Mad — yes, you would get mad once in a while — really mad — but it wasn't an everyday happening. Not, at least, since I've known you."

"The anger was inside," countered Jan, "all locked up in me. I was never a slammer and a banger — still the hostility was there. Now, dialed-in with Christ, there is no more of that . . . my head and heart are together."

By 1970, when Jan arrived in Pennsylvania, his Christian commitment knew a solid foundation. "I was startin' to turn myself around," he modestly reveals. "Just startin' . . . I say this 'cause dope was still a big factor in my life.

"I gotta confess to somethin' else . . . I was really insecure without that "grass". Back in Nebraska, Butch encouraged my attendance at a small, nondenominational, country church. I wanted to go with him, but I was so nervous — so scared of the people there. This is truly far-out . . . I'd have to go smoke a joint to get the nerve to try church. That's what I meant earlier in the book about dope bein' a crutch.

"But God understood . . . Jesus Christ died for weak sinners like me. So The Lord took me into his fold anyway and I'm still there . . . strugglin' and tryin' to be a better person."

The first test of Jan's newly-found direction, spiritually, came when Jay Opperman was fatally injured in the Knoxville Sprint Car crash.

"Wow, I was blown away by grief," he acknowledges. "Jay and I had talked for years about the possibility of one of us gettin' wasted in racing. In the event that it should happen, we pledged that the survivor would play it real cool . . . no tears, no regrets and no second thoughts.

"Like so many things, when it actually happened, I found it hard to keep my pledge. After some time, I finally got my head screwed on straight and figured out that God hadn't smashed the life out of Jay. Racing wasn't necessarily God's show . . . it was Jay's and mine. Sure, he let it happen . . . he let us go out there and drive, but he also gave us strong bodies and reasonably good heads to handle ourselves. We made the choice to race . . . I still choose to . . . God didn't say — you Oppermans, you're gonna be racers or else. So instead of plunging back into the occult, which was my first inclination, I dealt into Christianity in a greater fashion than ever before."

February 16, 1975 was an historic day . . . the last time around for a major automobile race on the old Florida Fairgrounds (Tampa) half-mile. One final fling for the IMCA Sprint Cars and fifty years of tradition ended. The track area, owned by Tampa University, was to serve other purposes . . . namely a conversion to an extensive athletic facility.

Opperman, a regular visitor to IMCA's annual "Winternational Sprints" since 1969, had just earned his second consecutive title in the event (1974 and 1975). Afterwards, we both sat with our backs against the scarred, concrete wall, that had for so long kept charging Sprint Cars out of the main grandstand. Evening's shadows lengthened around us and a squeaky record of Auld Lang Syne played over the public address system . . .

Should auld acquaintance be forgot,
And never brought to mind?
Should auld acquaintance be forgot,
And days of auld lang syne!
For auld lang syne, my dear,
For auld lang syne,
We'll take a cup o' kindness yet
For auld lang syne.

Over and over the mournful melody played, and down below

— the thrill of victory slightly tempered by the end of an important racing era — Jan and I visited quietly.

"Sure hate to see the ol' place go," he noted — staring out at the nearly empty infield. "Tampa's been good to me . . . some of my best races were here — some of this ol' bum's greatest Christian memories are also associated with days spent in Tampa."

"Yeah, I'll miss this red clay, too" I replied. "But Florida hasn't been all that good to me . . . my life sort of came apart here. So how about telling me something about this Christianity trip . . . I need a little help to get me going."

Immediately, Jan Opperman's eyes lit up and his voice gained new strength. "Christ will get you goin' . . . he's the man. Just listen to what he says. He'll help the weakest crud, pick up the worst dude and you're neither of these.

"Christianity is a love thing . . . that's what it's all about. The kind of love that means caring and understanding for others — even those who tear your guts out and hurt you so bad. Don't feel sorry for yourself, feel sorry for them. They're the losers . . . theirs is the heaviest trip.

"Hey brother," he continued, "you're probably like I used to always be. Wantin' to knock the heads off the dudes that cut you up. Well, that's the wrong show . . . Jesus didn't preach revenge; he talked about forgiving. You can't tear a man's head off to straighten him out. Smile at him . . . show him some love — you'll gain a lot more that way . . . believe me. It ain't ever gonna be easy; Christ never said it would be easy . . . it's just right. And look what they did to him . . . yet, up on that cross he didn't curse his enemies — he prayed for their forgiveness.

"Do you ever read the Bible?" Jan asked me. Reluctantly, I had to confess my lacking in that department.

"Try it . . . pick it up and give God's message a chance. You're a writer — you know good writing . . . stick your nose into the New Testament and you'll like what you see," he promised. The Bible is the real manual for happiness; the answers are all there. Nobody needs to want for an answer, just do a little reading and then follow that with some faith. Mostly that means faith in the Lord's judgment and faith in yourself to be both strong and brave enough to accept that judgment.

"I say try the New Testament, 'cause it's ageless. Written a long time ago, the words are just as useful today as when they were first spelled out. My favorite parts are I Corinthians 13 and I John 4 — they have continually helped me the most. They're love chapters . . . they help you relate to people — all kinds of people — and that is what I need to know. All of the chapters are good — each with its own special brand of guidance. I know you can find some words to help you through these tough times and other rough spells that may come later."

Nowadays, Jan Opperman's work has expanded beyond the realm of pushing down a heavy gas pedal with his Simpson Flame-proof racing shoe. He is a full-fledged Minister of the Gospel. Since that "swan song" day for Tampa's ancient Fairgrounds, I have heard Reverend Jan speak on numerous occasions about the merits of Christianity. Up in a chilly Williams Grove grandstand on an Eastern Sunday, in Pastor Dale Brooks' small East Tampa church . . . and there were other times when just the two of us were involved.

"Being a Minister of the Gospel may not mean very much to some people," Jan recently remarked to me. "But I've got news for them, it means everything to me . . . plenty more than when they used to call me the Dirt Track Champion of America.

"It's pretty simple really, I want to help people . . . poor, beaten down, messed up folks who can't get enough of their acts together — characters who are bent out of shape the way I once was. Don't get me wrong . . . I'm not one of those pushy preacher types, spoutin' Biblical phrases and screamin' about hell and damnation. No way, I'll be there if I'm needed . . . just like the time you came to me in Tampa. Nobody knows all the answers — I certainly don't. But I'll never send any hurtin' dude away, either . . . no matter how bad a cat he may or may not be."

Jan Opperman is a Christian all right. Quite likely he comes as close to earning his membership under the cross as anyone that I have ever known. He isn't joking about all men being his brothers and, most of all, "Oppie" forgives his enemies . . . even the worst of them. For Jan has truly perfected that blessed trait of defeating a clenched fist with a smile.

> *Love your enemies, bless them that curse you, do good to them that hate you, and pray for them which despitefully use you, and persecute you.*
>
> *Matthew 5:39*
>
> *and*
>
> *Only the brave know how to forgive . . . A coward never forgave; it is not in his nature.*
>
> *Laurence Stern*

Sprint Cars, USAC and Things

With the conclusion of the 1973 racing season, Jan was being acclaimed as the best Sprint Car driver any place east of a sunset. One writer — the highly-regarded Brock Yates — went further than that. "Jan Opperman just might be the greatest pure, guts-to-wall racer in the world today," he wrote in the December 1973 issue of Car and Driver magazine.

Ironically, '73 was not one of Opperman's better years . . . nothing like the preceding campaign. Although he, Bogar and Heintzelman won twenty-six features and were the Selinsgrove Speedway Champions . . . they had experienced their collective share of difficulties. Arch rival Kenny Weld — at the same time — powered to his best record ever. The Weld-Weikert crew garnered forty-three wins . . . one shy of Jan's fantastic victory mark, established in 1972.

No matter, "Opp" was the darling of motorsport's journalistic contingent. His zest for racing and personal warmth had won their ink-smeared hearts in much the same fashion as he had captured the enthusiasm of the fans, who jammed into splintery bleachers to cheer every move by this genuine American Folk Hero. Even the stuffy, stodgy Sports Car periodicals, heretofore considering Sprint Cars and the men who drove them to be profane objects, ran articles on Jan Opperman.

"Lookin' at that fancy writin' in the big magazines . . . it was hard to believe. Of course, all of the print was very flattering, but that didn't help Bogar's gang and me feel any better back there in '73. Heintzelman (his picture was rightfully in one of the magazines, also) tried everything, but nothin' worked," Jan recollects with only slight traces of disappointment. "Strangely, we were runnin' faster than the year before . . . better times and so forth. We just kept breakin' down . . . sailin' along like a rocket, then 'poof', somethin' would happen to the car.

"Kenny was goin' as good as we were bad and I was happy for him . . . winnin' meant a lot to Kenny. Me too . . . yet I have always known racin' is just like the rest of life. There are good days and bad days — good years and bad years — nobody is gonna change that. Therefore, I didn't pout and act like a spoiled brat . . . God doesn't like spoiled brats. I just praised God for the wins we did have and for bein' healthy and not gettin' hurt. Besides we were still winnin' our share."

Often overlooked by those who have typed out the words related to Opperman's life, is his undeniable contribution to Sprint Car design. In the winters . . . when snow drifted over the Pennsylvania ovals . . . Jan returned to Beaver Crossing, Nebraska. Like all racers in the area he spent considerable time visiting the shop, in nearby Lincoln, where noted builder, Don Maxwell, was headquartered. The end result of these off-season meetings was the eventual appearance of a fiendishly fast and different looking line of Sprinters.

"What we were tryin' to do, was build a car that was lighter, more slippery (lower in profile for aerodynamic purposes) and naturally with the motor clear back of center for dirt trackin'. We were strictly dirt track people . . . Don Maxwell, John Singer, Randy Hunt and a few others. Just a bunch of ol' clay racers, who figured — rightly or wrongly — that we had some answers," Opperman narrates. "Guess we were right, 'cause our cars sure worked."

Jan Opperman modestly continues: "However, don't call me a race car designer . . . I can't claim that title. I'm not even much of a mechanic; it takes people like Heintzelman or

Singer to keep me going . . . always did. Along with becoming a good driver, Maxwell was the designer-builder, and that's the truth.

"And John Singer is and was the best Sprint Car mechanic in the country — in my opinion. Some people disagree . . . chiefly 'cause he's had some severe personal problems and gets his head all screwed up from time to time. Singer is still the best.

"My contribution to the design was that I'd tramped all around the country racin' . . . here, there and everywhere. Boy, what a racin' tramp . . . but through it all I saw the best ideas in each place I went. Our car had some Heintzelman ideas, Trostle theories . . . quite a bit of Bobby Allen . . . heck it wasn't my design but instead the thinking of a whole army of men."

"All the same," I commented during this discussion, "I have heard plenty of 'inside' people refer to the type of machine, coming out of Maxwell's shop, as an Opperman chassis."

"That's all right, I suppose," answered Jan. "Personally, Maxwell chassis sounds better to me — more the way it should be.

"Let me say something about Sprint Car design and taking credit for same," he added. "No single person should take credit for an entire car-style . . . just part of it. In racin' everybody borrows from someone else's deal, makes some improvements and goes on. Except maybe an A.J. Watson . . . years ago, he was one of the first to hang a Sprinter on four torsion bars instead of springs. Trevis and all the others came along and made respective contributions. The present-day Sprint Car is a result of all this.

"Wait a minute," concludes Jan, "there is one dude over in Pennsylvania who oughta have some credit. Bobby Allen . . . now there's a mechanical genius. He moved up to Pennsylvania from Florida, knowin' very little about Sprints. Soon he was doin' things with chassis adjustment, weight distribution, and new metal uses that stood everyone on their ears. Allen has been a fine driver — steerin' the cars he builds — but he would've been unbeatable had he kept secret the things he knew. Not him . . . Bobby is a real decent guy and he shared his insight with his competitors. Hobos, like me, dragged Allen's tricks everywhere and the cars that Maxwell, Singer and I built in Lincoln were as much a credit to Bobby Allen as anyone else."

Call them Maxwells, Oppermans, Singers, or any name you choose — the new, low-nosed methanol eaters soon began to make their presence felt. Up front in the surging fields of America's dirt-tracking Sprinters, they quickly established themselves as money makers. Bill Smith, as well as many other Corn Belt car owners, took advantage of their potential and a few of the machines began to filter into California. The first of these vehicles to reach Pennsylvania was delivered in 1973 to a friend of Opperman's — Dr. Tom Houser* — a chiropractor from Watsontown (Pennsylvania). In the next couple of years there would be others, including the famed Al Hamilton Contracting Special, operating on the hotly-contested Keystone State racing scene, and this fact still pleases Jan no end.

"Regardless of designer name, I had helped with the thing and it was a tremendous treat to see our cars compete . . . especially that first one that "Doc" (Houser) bought to run at "The Groves"," Opperman reveals.

As a note of interest, Jan would eventually log some high-flying laps in the sleek Sprinters that he had helped to create. Driving for Bill Smith, John Aden and Al Hamilton . . . several of "Oppie's" finest triumphs were registered in vehicles which, in part, bore his name as builder . . . Maxwell, Opperman and Singer.

Meanwhile, back to the conclusion of the '73 dirt-track season and a dilemma that was developing for Jan Opperman. You have to know Jan to understand why there was a dilemma

*Unfortunately, Dr. Houser's racing career was short-lived. He died in 1975 — before his thirtieth birthday — of Hodgkin's disease.

at all. He was being referred to as the toughest Sprint Car racer in the land and some said he was the richest. Good enough . . . the credentials were there — one win at the Knoxville Nationals (1971), two victories at the world famous Western Championships in Phoenix (1971-72), and added to these were dozens of colorful wins picked up in his yearly, coast-to-coast attack upon the nation's earthen ovals.

Jan was a proud man; he had decimated his foes on the wind-raped prairie tracks, frequently crushed another horde of opponents on the meticulously manicured Pennsylvania dirt and beaten back the best competition afforded by a sun-bleached Southwestern circuit. Outlaw King . . . no doubt . . . but Jan Opperman was, nonetheless, afflicted with a malady that sooner or later overtakes every prominent member of the "renegade racer's fraternity". He hadn't proven himself on a regular basis with the United States Auto Club (USAC). To that organization's membership — a lofty group, at least — Opperman was just another outlaw, only with longer hair and a larger reputation. And, when you are a genuine USACer you use the word "outlaw" in a condescending fashion — generally accompanied by a sneer.

Perhaps some explanation is in order. USAC came to life in 1956, when its predecessor — The American Automobile Association — dropped all sanctioning of motor racing events because of the sport's increasing violence and rapidly growing casualty list.* Not only was the Indianapolis 500 left without a sanctioning agency, but so were all the many open-cockpit happenings (Midget, Sprint and Champ-Car) formerly directed by the A.A.A. So a handful of dedicated racing people put together the United States Auto Club. It's been a powerful force in our nation's motorsport picture ever since.

In the tradition of its organizational ancestor (AAA), USAC remained haughtily indignant in most judgments of non-

*1955 had been a very bloody year. Larry Crockett, Mike Nazaruk, Manuel Ayulo, Bill Vukovich, Jerry Hoyt and Jack McGrath (all established AAA open-cockpit stars) died in ghastly crashes. That was enough for the grand old racing club.

member drivers. Outlaws were just that — outlaws . . . men incapable of "cutting the mustard" within the Indianapolis based club.

For Sprint Car independents like Opperman, the United States Auto Club offered (and still does offer) two inducements to pay your dues and become a member. First of all, there is the fact of the Indianapolis Motor Speedway. If you want to run "The Brickyard" . . . well, supposedly competing with USAC's good ol' Sprint Car boys is one of the better ways to prove your worth for such an undertaking.

Secondly, there is the issue of pride. Though they don't like to admit it, many a hard-bitten outlaw buys into the USAC scheme of things because he gets darned sick of hearing . . . "He ain't bad but he ain't never made it with USAC."

Making the switch to United States Auto Club Sprint racing is a major step to men of Jan Opperman's ilk. Smaller schedules and smaller purses can mean reduced incomes for big winners such as Jan had been. No more $60,000 seasonal earnings. Also, USAC's "Thunder and Lightning" clan stages a good half of its programs on asphalt tracks . . . in some cases these are the steeply-banked, Midwestern speed bowls that dismember both drivers and cars with gusto. Such an experience can be nightmarish for gents long accustomed to the side-biting traction presented by Mother Earth's own soil.

But hold the phone, there is more to the USAC hassle. Reduced engine sizes (USAC permits no more than 305 cubic inches of displacement in its Sprint motors) necessitates severely altered driving styles . . . the unlimited power is just not present. And then there is the final nail to the coffin's lid. United States Auto Club officials frown on their drivers performing any high-speed heroics outside the organization's jurisdiction. Otherwise, it's do your racing with us or get out . . . be a good company man or tote your helmet bag elsewhere. Of course, exceptions are made — just not very often.

Hence, the dilemma for the free-spirited hippie, Jan

Opperman. In 1974, he chose the USAC fork in the trail and to this day he isn't sure why.

"Excuse my language, but it was a hell of a choice to make," Jan will tell you. "Through the outlaws, I'd gained some money for the first time in my life — some fame too. But talk is cheap — all the praising articles and so forth. The fact remained that there was an important bunch of guys (USAC) who didn't think I could drive my way 'round a hog lot. No, I've never been a glory hunter . . . however, I'm a competitor and the thought of this really freaked me.

"No doubt, I must admit also that I was startin' to get ideas about Indy. Every race driver does. Little did I know how quickly my chance would come there.

"Sure, I knew about the USAC hassle," Opperman notes. "There was a wagon load of hassle then . . . it's not so bad now. I had taken 'em on a couple of times before, with temporary permits — heard all the remarks about my long hair . . . the usual stuff. I also knew about the asphalt tracks; or rather I knew what I didn't know about them. Guess it was plainly a matter of confidence in myself . . . that I could do the job. Goin' USAC was probably just one of those trips — like so many others — that a dude has to take."

As Jan has stated, he had poured himself into the USAC "pressure cooker" on at least two other occasions. The first came in March of 1971.

"That's a day to forget," Jan acknowledges with a grin. "The car didn't work . . . it was really dialed out and so was the driver. We both stunk and those USAC characters, mostly car owners, laid on the needle. Some of 'em smiled at me and said not to feel bad . . . girls couldn't drive Sprint cars — they were for men only.

"My dad was with me and he got mighty sore. 'Jan, you oughta punch their lights out for sayin' that crap,' he said. I remember tellin' him that their lousy attitude was their problem — not mine. The words didn't hurt near so much as that insane-handling car and my crummy driving."

Opperman's next USAC Sprint attempt — over two years

later — was sung to a drastically different tune. June 24, 1973 . . . Jan driving for Dick Bogar was issued a temporary permit to compete in a United States Auto Club one-night stand at Williams Grove. The "Orange Box", equipped with a small motor, and Bogar's crew — decked out in shaggy hair, bib overalls and general hillbilly finery — were both ready.

With the dust finally settling around eleven P.M., Jan Opperman had set fast time (breaking the track record), won his heat and easily captured the feature. His only serious challenger was Kenny Weld, also running on a temporary permit. It goes without saying that very little discussion arose that evening pertinent to the subject of girls driving Sprint Cars.

"A whole lot was made about my beating USAC so badly," Jan observes. "It shouldn't have been . . . USAC cars are all-purpose machines, designed to run on dirt and pavement. They can never be a match for anything like Heintzelman's clay slinger. Plus, we knew the track much better . . . I heard how we were really flyin'. Not at all . . . I didn't have to and just stroked my way around the place. They did the flyin' but didn't go anywhere. We simply had too many advantages in our corner.

"I was particularly happy for Kenny. His brother had been a big USAC stud and some of the Indy folks were convinced that Ken was afraid to follow in Greg Weld's footsteps. Ol' Kenny showed those cats a thing or two that Sunday night. Considering all of our trouble, there was never anything "yellow" about Kenny Weld."

Consequently, when Jan Opperman and Dick Bogar's notorious gang showed up at Reading, Pennsylvania — March 24, 1974 — for the USAC Sprint opener, no introductions were necessary. The United States Auto Club gentry was already well acquainted with its new, long-haired, dues-paying member. Again, Opperman's dirt-tracking magic worked its spell . . . very nearly, that is. After a see-saw battle in the feature, Jan came away with a second place finish.

Exactly one week later, his face bloodied by a wheel-slung

rock, "Oppie" won the main event at Rossburg, Ohio's Eldora Speedway. This was a particularly bitter pill for the USACers to swallow. Eldora . . . the world's fastest half-mile dirt facility, because of its steep banking . . . was the closest thing to a home track, claimed by the nomadic USAC band. This time the advantage had been theirs and Jan Opperman blitzed that advantage into a clay-shrouded oblivion.

A faded-orange car bucking at breakneck speeds over Eldora's rutted hills; a blood-stained driver in the winner's circle . . . yet, somehow, USAC's greatest scare was still to come. Push the calendar ahead two more weeks. April 14 — Terre Haute, Indiana — USAC's richest Sprint Car race (The Hulman Classic) and ABC's Wide World of Sports cameras were on hand. So were the finest United States Auto Club drivers . . . A. J. Foyt, Gary Bettenhausen, George Snider, Sam Sessions — all of the celebrated names sparkling with the luster of Indianapolis and the grandeur of big-time auto racing.

His battered Levi jacket collar snapped tightly around his neck against a penetrating cold wind, Opperman was granted the prime interview time by ABC's Chris Economaki. A few moments later Jan wriggled into Dick Bogar's car and came within a cat's whisker of swiping all the marbles.

It was a titanic struggle, Gary Bettenhausen against Opperman. Once, near the event's conclusion, glancing through the tire-gouged holes, Jan powered around the front-running Bettenhausen and appeared headed for victory. However, simultaneously a spinning car brought out the yellow flag, nullifying the dramatic pass. A reversion to the original order occurred and that's the way they finished — Gary Bettenhausen first and "Oppie" second.

"That crazy Opperman," 1972 USAC Sprint Champ, Sam Sessions, later told me. "He really showed us something . . . really did make believers of us all."

Unfortunately, Jan Opperman's star, that had shone so brilliantly in the early spring, began to fade with warmer weather. Except, of course, for his scintillating performance at

The Indianapolis Motor Speedway, which will be covered in the next chapter.

For one thing, with the arrival of summer, the USAC Sprint Division's heart annually turns to pavement . . . the great dirt track rush is over. It was no different in 1974 and "Opp" was confronted by a legion of asphalt races, armed only with Bogar's faithful earth mover.

For another, Dick Bogar was growing tired of the continual long tows to the Midwest and financial problems were beginning to rear their ugly heads. Jan tried several other machines, chiefly John Aden's lavender-colored car — a Maxwell, Opperman, Singer chassis. The ride was fast — a one lap record set at Reading on July 3rd proved that. But fast isn't always enough in Sprint Car racing; a team's reliability is on the line as well. Mechanical woes, a costly spin at Eldora (July 13) . . . things weren't going well for the man in the fringed moccasins.

To make matters worse, an ever-widening rift was forming between Jan and the USAC officials. Russ Clendenen (Sprint Car Supervisor) objected to Opperman's wandering away to mid-week outlaw races. Plus, one of Jan's youthful crew members allegedly cursed Clendenen, with a substantial fine being the result. The conflict of interests reached a point of no return and Opperman — well beyond any love of hassling or being hassled — turned in his United States Auto Club Sprint license.

"I tried to explain to Mr. Clendenen," Jan relates. "I told him I was a professional racer, that USAC scheduling couldn't support me and occasional outlaw races were needed to make ends meet. From my point of view there seemed little harm in running a Nebraska show (or somewhere) on a Wednesday night.

"He disagreed . . . he told me that rules were rules . . . if I insisted upon runnin' outside the club, others would expect the same treatment. I could understand that . . . he had a point. Just the same, my situation was bad. Rules might be rules, but they wouldn't feed my family or make property payments. There were no particular hard feelings on my part . . . I was just a racer who had to look after himself."

Back to the outlaws he went. Back where there were neither rules nor asphalt-plated tracks. Throughout the remainder of 1974 and for the entire duration of 1975, Jan took only an occasional shot at USAC sanctioned programs (never Sprint Cars). Many of his old rivals, hard-core USACers to the bitter end, considered him to be washed up — burned out. One of them, whose name we will respectfully omit, put it to me this way:

> "I don't know about Jan — he was in, even at Indy. Now look at him — off runnin' meaningless races at nowhere tracks. Nope — I sure don't know about Jan . . . he's just wasting away his life."

Dead and buried, that's where they had Jan Opperman. Off in some God-forsaken boothill cemetery for desperado race drivers, where he would never be heard from again. Hardly . . . in 1976 "the champion of the meaningless race circuit" returned from "nowhere" and — you guessed it — moved back into USAC's domain with a heavier foot than before. 1976 — the year of America's Bicentennial; the year that Jan Opperman rose to the front as a full-fledged United States Auto Club hero.

"Bein' thirty-seven years old kind of made it a now or never proposition," Jan presents as an explanation for his return to USAC. "Bill Smith — my old boss from Nebraska — offered the car; one that Maxwell, Singer and I had put together earlier. Plus, I had a Speedway (Indianapolis) deal cookin' . . . so back to USAC once again."

The car, painted outlaw black and wearing number sixty-four, was a fierce one . . . a genuine smoke 'em off beast on anybody's dirt track. Even so, Opperman played it real cool at first; no wild moves and no risky bits of strategy. He finished a comfortable sixth in the opener at Eldora (March 28) and returned to the same track for a second on April 11.

A sigh of relief whistled through the United States Auto

Club battalion — that cross-wearing hippie seemed to have settled down.

Next came Terre Haute's Hulman Classic, with a record purse predicted. The same event where Jan's brilliant drive had fallen short two years before. He timed in fifth fastest, won his heat and started outside front row — next to old pal Bubby Jones — in the feature.

At the green, Opperman rushed into the lead . . . driving aggressively on the loose cushion, deep within the hulking shadow of the outer guard rail. What a ferocious exhibition . . . elbows and arms slashing and wrenching the steering wheel — mud plastered all over man and car . . . Jan's speeds appeared to increase with each lap. At times, he hardly seemed to breathe the engine in the turns — preferring to allow it to scream at maximum revolution potential.

Behind him came USAC's most brutal competitor — Duane "Pancho" Carter, Jr. Carter, a super driver, was frantic — utterly desperate to run down Opperman. With an awesome display of bravery, "Pancho" turned Steve Stapp's pale-blue car inside out in his urgency. Smack into the third turn wall, crunch into the fourth turn concrete — Carter kept on coming. Up on two wheels, a shower of clay chunks surrounding his entire trail . . . the relentless pursuit continued.

" 'Pancho' is gonna kill himself tryin' to catch Jan," an anguished Carter crew member moaned.

Fortunately, this never happened. The checkered flag fell; Jan had led all forty laps and earned $12,000 for his wire to wire run to Wabash Valley glory. The cautious, real-cool playing was over.

Afterwards — in the pits, with great thunderclouds looming off turn three — Opperman could scarcely conceal his jubilation.

"Far out . . . Praise God," he exclaimed. "These USAC guys didn't think a bunch of Nebraska hayseeds could win such a big race, but I knew we were ready — we were hooked up. Hayseeds don't win or lose races . . . motors, tires and The

Almighty have charge of winnin' and losin'. Praise God for all this."

A short distance down the pit lane, "Pancho" Carter felt no such joy. In an attempt to vent a super-charged frustration, he assaulted his steaming mount with both fist and foot. Finally, exhausted by the physical and emotional on-the-track ordeal he had been through, "Pancho" sat against a stack of tires to stare placidly at Opperman's victory celebration.

Since a complete chronological listing of Jan's 1976 USAC racing record follows this particular chapter, little more needs to be detailed on the subject. That is, with the exception of one final significant fact. In June, Opperman got the greatest break of his United States Auto Club career. He was hired, as a driver, by Bobby Hillin of Midland, Texas.

Hillin — a Texan to the hilt, wearing an enormous hat and Tony Lama boots — had been a road racing enthusiast, who somehow became interested in USAC-style, oval racing. He owned a stable of handsome bronze-colored machines, running under the label of Longhorn Racers and wrenched by a bearded behemoth — Donnie Ray Everett.

Hiding beneath the layers of metal-flake paint were some mighty fine pieces of speed equipment — a Champ-Dirt Car, two Sprinters and eventually even an Indy Car was added to the collection.

With a steady diet of asphalt races lurking amidst the coming weeks, Bobby Hillin's Sprint Cars proved invaluable to Opperman. His assigned vehicle was the number six . . . built by Steve Stapp and totally adjustable from dirt tracks to paved surface racing.

"It wasn't as good on dirt as my other rides had been," Jan elaborates, "but it was far better on pavement. That's what

Author's Note: As an added note of interest, Chuck Gurney was flipped out of the track on The 1976 Hulman Classic's final lap. After taking the checkered flag, Opperman came upon the scene. Stopping his own car, Jan vaulted the crash barrier and rushed to the aid of the screaming Gurney, who was being cooked by his own spilling oil. Chuck Gurney was pulled free of the overturned machine by Opperman. A few months later, these same two drivers would be reunited by another accident — the disaster described in this book's opening chapter.

you need in USAC . . . flexibility, and The Longhorn machine was my first chance at all-purpose equipment."

This was well established on August 22 at Dayton, Ohio. The Dayton half-mile is one of those feared speed bowls, found only in the Midwest, that strangles courage from the boldest men. Opperman won that day, narrowly defeating Carter — who like his father before him — seems to thrive on the ghoulish "Hills of death", as they are often called. That Jan Opperman victory was his first ever on a paved course, while driving Sprint Cars with USAC.

In retrospect, Jan views The United States Auto Club, its membership and his relationship to both, far less acrimoniously than he once did.

"I'm an outlaw . . . I'll always be that way . . . a dude that has to try his own thing, no matter what. Organizations, as you know, aren't my bag — nope, they sure aren't. Yet, you gotta have respect for USAC . . . all that tradition and pride. I can really relate to pride. So long as pride is earned and USAC has earned the right to feel proud," Jan says, a touch of reverence in his voice.

"At one time I thought all USACers were stuck-up, snotty dudes. That's not so. Yeah, some of the car owners were a little that way and ol' Russ Clendenen gave me some problems. Not the drivers . . . they're just ordinary racers doin' their best. Some of my closest racing friends have belonged to the club . . . Rich Leavell, Bubby Jones and, of course, James McElreath. And don't let me forget Sam Sessions. Sammy is gone now — killed in a snowmobile last year (1977) — but he was a peach of a man. He helped me — befriended me and there was nothin' snotty about Sammy. An old-guard USAC cat all the way . . . Sessions never hassled the first person.

"Don't let anyone tell you otherwise, The United States Auto Club is a big part of American auto racing."

So sayeth the grandest outlaw of them all and nobody knows the story better than he. Jan Opperman has been among the best of both worlds.

OPPERMAN DROVE EXTENSIVELY IN ALL FOUR USAC OPEN-COCKPIT DIVISIONS DURING 1976. HERE, EXCLUDING INDIANAPOLIS CARS, ARE HIS TOP FINISHES.

SPRINTS

Date		Track	Surface	Finish	Car	
Mar.	28	Eldora Speedway	1/2 mile dirt	6th place	Bill Smith Speedway Motors Special	
Apr.	11	Eldora Speedway	1/2 mile dirt	2nd place	Bill Smith Speedway Motors Special	
May	1	Terre Haute Action Track	1/2 mile dirt	1st place	Bill Smith Speedway Motors Special	
June	4	Indiana Fairgrounds	1 mile dirt	4th place	Bill Smith Speedway Motors Special	
June	11	Schererville, Indiana	1/2 mile paved	7th place	Longhorn Racers	
July	3	Findlay, Ohio	1/2 mile dirt	7th place	Longhorn Racers	
July	10	Eldora Speedway	1/2 mile dirt	1st place	Longhorn Racers	
July	11	New Bremen, Ohio	1/2 mile paved	2nd place	Longhorn Racers	
July	16	Schererville, Indiana	1/2 mile paved	5th place	Longhorn Racers	
July	17	Toledo, Ohio	7/16 mile paved	9th place	Longhorn Racers	
July	31	Indiana Fairgrounds	1 mile dirt	2nd place	Longhorn Racers	Two events
July	31	Indiana Fairgrounds	1 mile dirt	6th place	Longhorn Racers	in one evening
Aug.	6	Schererville, Indiana	1/2 mile paved	5th place	Longhorn Racers	
Aug.	7	Eldora Speedway	1/2 mile dirt	3rd place	Longhorn Racers	
Aug.	22	Dayton, Ohio	1/2 mile paved	1st place	Longhorn Racers	
Aug.	27	Hamburg, New York	1/2 mile dirt	3rd place	Longhorn Racers	

*Hoosier Hundred injuries prevented any further competition in 1976. He was fifth in points at the time of the accident.

MIDGETS

June 30	Clermont, Indiana	5/8 mile paved	4th place	Bob Lithgow Special
July 7	Kokomo, Indiana	1/4 mile dirt	5th place	Bob Lithgow Special
July 14	Clermont, Indiana	5/8 mile paved	2nd place	Bob Lithgow Special
Aug. 8	Dayton, Ohio	1/2 mile paved	1st place	Bob Lithgow Special
Aug. 14	Trenton, New Jersey	1.5 mile paved	4th place	Howard Linne Special
Aug. 18	Clermont, Indiana	5/8 mile paved	1st place	Bob Lithgow Special
Aug. 20	Springfield, Illinois	1/4 mile dirt	1st place	Bob Lithgow Special
Sept. 6	Gardena, California	1/2 mile dirt	1st place	Shefchik Special

*Opperman, who had been a long time away from Midgets, had phenomenal success in 1976 — winning four of his last five starts.

CHAMPIONSHIP DIRT

*Jan's record in the big dirt cars is misleading. In each of the three 100-Milers offered, prior to his accident, he ran with the front-runners — only to be plagued by misfortune.

Aug. 21	Springfield, Illinois	1 mile dirt	Ran out of fuel on lap 88 while leading the race.
Aug. 29	DuQuoin, Illinois	1 mile dirt	Jan started twentieth — was in second place on lap 46, when he was forced to the side-lines by mechanical problems.
Sept. 11	Indiana Fairgrounds	1 mile dirt	Crashed while attempting to pass leader.

All rides in The Longhorn Racers Hook'em II Car.

The Indy Experience

I don't care for contemporary Championship Cars or Indy Cars — regardless of which nomenclature someone chooses to assign them. I've never liked the space-aged machines . . . not since the first of their ancestors immigrated to these shores back about 1961. Champ Cars — especially today's highly refined variety — tend to emulate the appearance of working models for the first supersonic, celestial vacuum cleaners. When watching them compete, I feel as though I'm living amidst "Future Shock" or, at least, having a close-enough encounter with some unknown species.

This isn't Jan Opperman speaking, but instead these words represent the prejudice of his biographer . . . a dirt track purist 'til the last chunk of clay has crumbled into dust. If there is anything the Indy machines — along with their supporting human element — fail to comprehend, it's dirt. The slightest trace of such a hostile substance, upon any of their billiard table-smooth playgrounds, will quickly send one or more of the blue-blood racers spinning away to a shattering date with the concrete.

But give the Champ Cars their proper due. They go so fast that "hell wouldn't have 'em". In all likelihood, excluding straight-running dragsters, these are the fastest four-wheeled vehicles in the world. So speedy are they that hardcore Indy people continually argue the merits of slowing them down for the sake of safety. The arguments may rage but the Indianapolis Cars are oblivious to political strife . . . they just keep going faster.

It's tough for an old reprobate from the mud and grime circuits — such as this writer — to describe a prime specimen of USAC Championship equipment. They're so "far out" — so expensive that you hate to snuggle up next to one for the purpose of getting acquainted. You might scratch it or leave greasy fingerprints on a waxy paint job.

There are several things, however, that come to mind. The "champers" do their traveling on squat, pudgy tires and ride so close to the ground that a sausage pizza would have to be rolled extra thin to fit between their flat bellies and the asphalt. Of course, engines are located to the rear — behind the driver — and are usually turbocharged.

The men who build these land-roving missiles love to attach weird names to their exotic bits of mechanical creativity. Things like Lotus, Lola, Eagle, Scorpion, Wildcat, Dragon and Lightning . . . obviously some of the more potent members of our natural fauna are favorite choices.

The most unique feature of all has to do with driving technique. Unlike Sprint Cars which feature plenty of arm and elbow action, combined with neck-whipping violence — the rear-engined, pavement prowlers present little driver activity at all. So far as an observer can see, that is. Why . . . because drivers virtually lie down in the narrow cockpits, only the tops of their brightly-decorated helmets being visible. Also, there had better not be too much arm and elbow action by Champ-Car chauffeurs, since the tricky machines have fat, compact steering wheels which attach to very sensitive steering systems. Too much arm and elbow action will most assuredly relieve some Indy tycoon of his $100,000 and up investment and only God can help the driver, even if he survives. Indianapolis-style racing is two hundred miles per hour living in a pressure cooker . . . desperate, dangerous, computerized and definitely "big bucks". So what . . . every open-cockpit race driver, worth the price of his nomex underwear, wants a part of it. Some will sell their souls; others donate life and limb . . . simply to gain admission to the jet-propelled merry-go-round.

Despite the term Indy Car, which is justly deserved through association with the Indianapolis 500, "in-the-know" race fans realize that USAC's heralded Championship Division has a season-long schedule that it supports. Appropriately dubbed "The Championship Trail", the routine used to include two other 500 milers (Ontario, California and Pocono, Pennsylvania) and a host of shorter races*. Foreign countries have even been visited in recent years . . . Canada, Argentina, Japan, and in 1978, England's green countryside will hear the shrieking wail of America's famed Indy machinery.

All the same, The Indianapolis Motor Speedway gives the division a real reason for existence. Truthfully, the United States Auto Club, in its entirety, is closely linked with the place that racers respectfully refer to as The Speedway. Two and one-half miles of glistening pavement that covers the original brick surface (3,200,000 bricks to be exact) that greeted the first Indy 500 in 1911.

Indy is many things . . . The Purdue University Band, naked college kids rolling in a muddy infield, the tension-packed voice of announcer Tom Carnegie, 400,000 screaming fans, massive traffic jams, horrid crashes and unrivaled acts of bravery. Most significantly, it has long remained the ultimate test and goal for race drivers. Jan Opperman, the "Thank God I'm a Country Boy" hippie from Nebraska, was no different. The same dream had frequently taunted him. Could he make it — could he run The Speedway?

*Regular stops include: FasTrack International Speedway (Phoenix, Arizona), Trenton International Speedway (Trenton, New Jersey), Wisconsin State Fair Speedway (Milwaukee), Michigan International Speedway (Brooklyn, Michigan) and Texas World Speedway (College Station, Texas). The shortest are Phoenix and Milwaukee at one mile in length. Michigan and Texas are the longest at two miles, while Trenton measures out to a mile and a half.

"Fisher's[1] Folly", "Hulman's[2] Speed Palace" . . . the world's most famous race course abounds with nicknames and is well oiled by clever cliches and other tidbits of journalistic jargon. So much has been either written or said about The Indianapolis Motor Speedway, that quite honestly there appears to be little virgin territory left on the subject. Yet there is one aspect to the personality of the sacred Indianapolis acreage, located at the corner of West Sixteenth Street and Georgetown Road, that can hardly be emphasized enough. The reference here is being made to The Speedway's traumatic impact upon the lives of the men who dare to take it on. A legend in its own concrete, steel and asphalt self . . . The Speedway, nonetheless, has the power to both manufacture and crush flesh and bone legends. Few man-made structures carry that kind of clout.

When Jan Opperman first showed up at Indy in 1974, his legendary status was already well established. He was rather unique in that sense . . . one of the few American open-cockpit racers to achieve such prominence without benefit of Indianapolis exposure. And yet, somehow, in his two flings to date at "the big casino", Jan's reputation received further enhancement. Again a touch of the unusual is registered, for Opperman never won the race nor did he ever lead a single lap.

The following pages tell the story of Jan Opperman's colorful relationship with The Indianapolis Motor Speedway. A story of last-second time trailing, indescribable audacity and grandiose displays of courage. A story told primarily in Jan's very words.

1974

"Tell me," I asked "Opp", while making the tapes for our manuscript, "did Parnelli Jones really make you get a haircut

[1] Carl Fisher — automotive pioneer, industrialist, and real estate speculator — built The Speedway on farmland west of Indianapolis, in 1909.

[2] Anton "Tony" Hulman purchased The Speedway prior to the 1946 Race. It was he that renovated the grounds and introduced the place to its contemporary image.

before he would allow you to drive his Indy Car in 1974?"

"Yeah . . . uh, definitely — he made me get a haircut. But let me tell you how it all happened," Opperman answered.

"The floor is yours — all yours." was my reply.

"Well, I was runnin' a USAC Sprint show (5/5/74) at that Cincinnati paved track. My ride was a regular USAC car — a little light in horsepower, but a good handling machine just the same.

"After the race Sammy Sessions came up to me. I've already told you how much I thought of Sam . . . he was an outlaw racer once and he always made me feel real welcome with USAC. Anyway, he said, 'Opperman, what do you think about Indianapolis?'

"I told him that I didn't think too much about it — no more than any dirt trackin' drifter could. I had never seen the place. Neither had I ever seen an Indy Car, except on television or in pictures. Of course The Speedway had been sort of a goal but right then it seemed a long way off.

"Sessions told me, 'Maybe not, Jan . . . you're good, plenty good enough to go to Indianapolis. Why don't you come over to The Speedway tomorrow? I've got some connections* . . . I'll introduce you around and we'll see if we can land you a Champ Car ride.'

"Wow, did that ever make me feel good. Sammy sure did blow me away with all that praise and I agreed to meet him in the Speedway's garage area, the next morning.

"Boy, I really appreciated what Sessions was offering to do for me, 'cause I didn't know anybody on the Indy scene. The next morning I hustled right on over to the track and just like he had promised, Sam was waiting at his garage. He really treated me great. We went all

*Sammy Sessions surely did have some connections. Before retiring from Champ Car racing, after the '75 season, Sam would compete in seven Indy 500 Mile Races. His best finish was a fourth in 1972.

around the place and Sammy introduced me to each of the insiders that he knew. My little girl, Krystal, was with me at that time, and she just trucked along beside her dad. Must have been quite a sight . . . an ol' long hair and his baby daughter mixin' in with America's most important racing folks. If you remember . . . I mentioned earlier about usually travelin' with one or more of my kids, in order to stay close to them.

"As I was being introduced around, I finally spotted a guy that I had met previously. He was Johnny Capels, a former Sprint driver from Albuquerque, and now a chief mechanic with Parnelli Jones' racing team.

"Just before seeing Capels, at work on one of Parnelli's cars, I had pretty well decided to leave, bein' as neither Sessions nor I had hit on any possibilities for me. This was Monday and I had to be out in Lincoln, Nebraska to drive for Bill Smith on Wednesday night. But when I spied Johnny, I figured I might as well wander in and say hello. That was my reason for coming to The Speedway in the first place . . . to make as many contacts as possible.

"Capels and I greeted each other and visited a few minutes. There was another man in the garage and Capels introduced us. It turned out to be Vel Miletich — Parnelli Jones' partner in the Champ Car team. We shook hands and I liked him instantly. Vel looks you right in the eye when talking and he is not one of those fancy conversationalists who can't ever seem to call a spade a spade. He just gets right down to business.

" 'I hear you are a darn good race driver,' he said to me.

" 'Yeah, I guess . . . I work at it pretty hard,' was my reply. 'I know I'm not too pretty (long hair, Levis and a tee shirt hardly represented the Indy image) but I can drive all right.'

"Then I gathered up some courage and made the big move. Knowing that the team had an extra car because

Joe Leonard* — one of their regular drivers — had been injured . . . I launched into my pitch. 'If you need another driver for the spare racer, I'd sure like a chance . . . I'm positive that I can drive one of these things.

"Vel didn't say anything for a second and then he sighted me in. 'Hey — you know what — I believe you. I believe you can drive one of our cars too, but we'll have to wait until Parnelli gets back tomorrow (Tuesday) afternoon. He makes all of the decisions about drivers. You come back tomorrow,' he said, 'and we can talk to Parnelli. If he agrees, you're hired.'

"As Vel Miletich had suggested, I returned to The Speedway on Tuesday. Sammy Sessions was still taking me around to the various garages when word reached me that Parnelli was back. So I excused myself and headed over to his garage to meet him.

"Parnelli told me that Vel had spoken to him about me and that he was interested. 'I'll hire you on one condition,' he stated. 'You've got to get a haircut . . . you have too much hair. Let me explain . . . I don't care about your hair length one bit, but my sponsors (Viceroy and Firestone) do. They insist upon a certain image and it's a pretty high-class one at that. So it's up to you.'

"I never hesitated a bit and agreed to get the haircut. It seemed a cheap price to pay for driving a super race car like that. No, it didn't make me mad . . . Parnelli was just tryin' to run his outfit according to the rules laid down by the sponsors. It was easy enough to understand . . . thousands and thousands of dollars were involved in a deal like that. Also, I mentioned to Parnelli about my Sprint Car commitment in Lincoln, Nebraska, the following evening. 'I never break a commitment for any reason,' I explained. He understood and told me to get back as soon as possible. Meanwhile they would start

*This had been auto racing's famed super team, with three famous drivers under wraps — Mario Andretti, Al Unser and Leonard.

gettin' the car ready. In turn I promised to return with a haircut and be ready to begin work by Friday, at the latest.

"Krystal and I piled into our car and drove all night (it takes twelve hours) to Beaver Crossing. After getting some rest, Mary Lou gave me a haircut. She really spruced me up . . . trimmed up my sideburns and whacked three or more inches off my mane. We thought I looked great, really sanitary and clean. That night I went out to Midwest Speedway and drove Bill Smith's Sprinter to a win.

"When I got back to Indianapolis — new haircut and all — I went right over to Parnelli's headquarters. He took one look at me and said, 'Not good enough . . . you've got to cut off more than that.' He was still bein' very nice about it, so I headed across the street to a barber shop . . . the first barber shop that had seen my shadow in years. The barber did some more trimming, styled my hair so it could be combed and then I headed back to the track. This time I passed inspection.

"Within a few minutes I had my new red and white uniform on and was helpin' to push the car toward the pit area. A short time after that I was motoring around the track . . . trying to learn the tricks of a rear-engined machine. Man, was I nervous. I gripped the wheel so tight that my hands and arms were exhausted. But everything worked out all right and after a couple of days I had passed the rookie test and was ready to qualify."

Again, in the opinion of his biographer, Jan Opperman's modesty tends to underplay his accomplishment. Having never driven a rear-engined car prior to May 10, 1974 and with nearly as little experience on asphalt — Jan's remarkable success in the Jones-Miletich car needs further description. He sailed through his rookie test almost effortlessly. On a horribly windy Sunday (May 12), Opperman completed the test, utilizing less than two days to familiarize himself with that particular car and Champ Cars in general. It is inconceivable that anyone could have done better.

There is also the matter of the car itself. Number fifty-one — the Viceroy Special — was hardly a picture of fine-handling perfection. Designed by Maurice Phillippe (previously a designer for Lotus Inc. of England), the vehicle was unique in that it was constructed with left-hand fuel tanks only — the first of its kind at Indy. Although the machine had performed well in mile-track competition, The Speedway transformed it into a treacherous beast whose ill-handling reputation soon spread throughout the garage area. Originally there had been three of the Phillippe creations but Al Unser and Mario Andretti gladly parked their steeds in favor of two of the more reliable Dan Gurney Eagles. Thus, it remained for Jan Opperman to wrestle with the only-surviving remnant of Maurice Phillippe's dream.

"Yeah, that fifty-one car — the Phillippe creation — was sort of a rat . . . a real rat, to be truthful," Opperman recalls. "It had extreme handling conditions at either end of the fuel load. When the tanks were full of fuel it wanted to hang the tail drastically — the thing was terribly loose. Then after the tanks emptied down, the car's front end would start pushin' like crazy. Actually, the only stable runnin' time was at the midway point of the fuel capacity.

"Two days before I was to qualify (Thursday, May 15) that brute caught up with me and we thumped the wall. The car got damaged and was barely repaired for time trials. With so little time to dial her in again, we could do no better than 176.186 m.p.h. for our four lap average. This gave us starting spot number thirty-two, which was very disappointing.

"In the race I got up to ninth or tenth before I popped a tire and spun the thing. Some people said I was really a "hot dog" — passin' all those cars. Not at all . . . I drove the corners badly and made some mistakes. The car was an animal to drive, but it had a great motor . . . a super motor. After strugglin' through the turns, that engine would take hold down those straightaways. Nobody had a stronger motor and we ate up a lot of competition on the straight stretches.

"Capels was truly a great help. He was capable of settin' the chassis and the wings to run at about any speed you wanted to go — even with the car's bad-handling traits. And Parnelli Jones was also very instrumental in my success. I wouldn't say Parnelli and I were close friends, but my association with him meant a lot to me. He said things to me about Champ Cars that made more sense than anything I've heard since."

As he said, Jan started the 1974 "500" in next to last starting spot (thirty-second). By lap eighty-five, he was in tenth and rapidly gaining on the ninth place car. At that time, a tire blew and spun into the grass between turns three and four. Desperate to restart, Opperman was sidelined when the remaining tires went flat at the scene of his calamity. A wrecker hauled the disabled machine back to the pits, which permanently ended Jan Opperman's rookie effort at the Indianapolis 500. Indy rules forbid an immobile car — towed to the pit area — from re-entering the race. Four damaged tires clearly constituted immobility and Jan's official finishing position was listed as twenty-first.

1976

1975 saw Opperman a long way removed, literally and figuratively, from the venerable USAC Champ Car scene. But in 1976 he was back for another fling at the earth-bound, piston-driven meteors. During that season, Jan would drive three different racers . . . The Mergard Eagle, The Routh Meat Packing Special and The Longhorn Racing Eagle. In the Routh car — a one-shot deal — he was once again to know the glory of Indianapolis 500 competition. The "believe it or not" relationship between Dick Routh, Jan Opperman and the world's greatest speedway provides most of the print for the concluding portion of this chapter.

When Chief Steward Tom Binford officially opened the Indy grounds for practice on May 8, Opperman's name was carried on the entry list as the pilot of Don Mergard's ancient Eagle. Definitely a low-budget enterprise, the Mergard team — including Jan — could not get the car up to a satisfactory speed. Things looked bleak for "Oppie" who was by then calling Noxon, Montana his home.

Bleakness was not confined to the Mergard aggregation, however. In another part of Gasoline Alley, Dick Routh's crew — headed by Todd Gibson* — was also encountering difficulties. Forced to rebuild their mount after a devastating crash at Trenton only a few weeks before Speedway time, the Ohio-based boys simply could not get the red, white and blue car to perform properly. They had a good enough driver . . . the experienced and talented Steve Krisiloff. Still the combination could not click. Eventually, Krisiloff — beset by frustration — took off for greener pastures and ended up qualifying another machine for the '76 "500". Immediately, he was replaced in the cockpit by Jerry Karl. New driver or not, practice lap speeds remained too slow for serious consideration.

Meanwhile back to Opperman. By some stroke of good fortune, he was able to coax a 180.045 m.p.h. average out of his wheezing vehicle to qualify on Sunday, May 16. The time was slow — terribly slow — but at least he was temporarily in the field. The question was . . . could his speed hold up or would faster cars bump him from the lineup during the next qualifying weekend? Most Speedway observers felt Jan's presence in the starting field would be short-lived. 180.045 was simply not fast enough.

Once again Jan Opperman's words will pick up the dialogue and relate the dramatic happenings that unfold in the ever-

*Todd Gibson had been one of America's all-time greats in asphalt Supermodified and Sprint Car racing. Also an excellent mechanic, he was crew-chiefing for Dick Routh in 1976. After Indy, Gibson — a native of Richwood, Ohio — took over the driving duties of the mount. He continued in his dual role until a 1977 crash at Michigan International Speedway sidelined both him and the car.

continuing saga of auto racing's resident miracle worker from "The Big Sky Country".

"Boy, '76 was a hairy deal. When we got Mergard's car up to 180, I knew we had done the very best we could do with it. Still, I honestly believed — slow as the time was — we would be in the show. There weren't that many characters runnin' much faster.

"Then somethin' happened that changed my mind. On Friday — right before the last time trial weekend — it rained in the morning and washed down the track. Next a red-hot sun came out. After the track dried, practice sessions began and that boilin' asphalt started pickin' up rubber off the tires. With all that good traction, speeds started going up. Uh-oh, I thought to myself . . . things weren't looking so good. But it was too late to do anything about it then. We were stuck with our time; plus there was no more speed in the car.

"All day Saturday I watched the various people and cars qualifying and more than ever I was worried. Plain enough, I was in trouble — when Saturday ended the field was full and we were still in. Just barely . . . ours was the slowest time . . . we were the next to be bumped. Worst of all, there was still Sunday — a whole day of timing — with some pretty sanitary outfits in line to run.

"That night I called some friends of mine, who were well hooked-up with God, to pray for me. Namely Reverend Dale Brooks in Tampa and Grandma Selmer up in Heron, Montana. Both of them said, 'Don't worry about it, Jan. You're gonna be in the race for sure . . . The Lord will see to it.'

"That made me feel better. Those people are really into prayer and if they had that kind of faith, then I could catch it too. You know . . . faith is really contagious. So on Sunday morning I went over to the track, fairly confident that I'd be in the show. Boy, did I blow a deal then. The first guy I saw in the garage area was Bobby Olivero. He was tryin' to make his first 500 —

he's just a young kid — and he was really cryin' the blues. Chiefly because his car was the next slowest after mine and second in line to be bumped.

" 'Oh Jan — man, we're going to be bumped for sure,' Olivero groaned.

"Never thinkin' about what Dale and Grandma might have meant, I started trying to cheer him up. 'No-No,' I told him, 'I've been in touch with some people of God who claim I'll be in the show. You've got a better time than I do . . . if I'm in, you will be too.'

"Olivero felt better until the first car out (driven by Tom Bigelow) bumped me and soon afterward Lloyd Ruby's time erased him. The Kid was sick, practically in tears. 'You said we were safe, that God was gonna look after us,' he said. I didn't know what to say then. Actually there wasn't anything to say . . . we were both out and that was that. A little later I found out that Grandma and Dale had been right . . . I would be in the show. Just in a different car. But it was too late to help Bobby — I felt way worse for him than I did for me. That poor kid was heartbroken and I hadn't helped matters any. Me and my big mouth.

"I wasn't feelin' too swift either . . . just ready to pitch the whole thing. There was a Sprint Car race at Findlay, Ohio and I told my crew (the members of which were hanging around the Speedway) to get the car ready. We had time to make it over there and earn a few bucks anyway. Mostly — bein' so fed up — I wanted to get in that Sprinter and use up my hostility on a good ol' dirt track.

"Now get this. I was the boss of the crew. But my Sprint mechanic, Terry Otero (Praise God for him) argued with me. 'No Jan, we're gonna stay here and you're gonna find another ride at this joint,' he told me. How about that? I'm supposed to be the boss and "Mexican" (Terry Otero's nickname) is tellin' me what to do."

Today, Jan Opperman can chuckle about his youthful

mechanic's blessed act of defiance. However, on May 23, 1976 there was little time for chuckling. The last-minute ride seeker at Indy is a desperate creature, running from garage to garage and up and down the qualification line, trying to get into someone's theretofore unsuccessful machine. It is an unenviable situation in which to find yourself. The best you can expect is to obtain permission to drive a car, discarded by another driver, with zero practice time available.

"I started hustling around, as Terry insisted, but nothing was available. All of a sudden a phone call came for me in Don Mergard's garage. It was a friend, Wink Bridges, from Champaign, Illinois. He told me that he (Mr. Bridges) would put up $10,000 cash if A. J. Foyt would let me drive the Foyt backup car. So, off to Foyt's garage I went. A. J. was very nice, but explained that he had too small a crew to maintain two cars.

"By then I was really frustrated. Again I hunted up "Mexican" and told him we were goin' Sprint Car racin'. Otero still disagreed. He insisted that I keep scratchin' around for some kind of deal. Feeling pretty "bum-kicked", I decided to take a hike down pit row where five or six cars were lined up for timing.

"I was just walkin' along, talkin' to The Lord, mumbling and jabbering to myself — trying' to get my head together — when this older guy yelled at me. He introduced himself as Dick Routh, the owner of one of the cars in the line waiting to be qualified. Routh told me how much he had always admired my stand on Christianity and prayer and that I should keep up my work with other folks in both respects. 'That's right-on stuff, mighty good stuff,' he said.

" 'How you doin' with your car?' I asked him.

" 'Bad,' he replied, 'we're going nine miles an hour too slow to make the program.'

" 'If you keep having trouble, can I get a chance with it?' I questioned.

" 'Yeah," Routh answered, 'we would love to have you,

but I've got to give Jerry Karl one last opportunity with the car. He's worked hard for us and deserves that.' "

Thus it was that Jan Opperman, his spirits slightly rejuvenated, trudged off to wait near Dick Routh's garage for Jerry Karl's luck to either improve or remain tainted. A few minutes later Routh sought him out and announced that Karl was still too slow. However, he had decided to go one more run with the Manchester, Pennsylvania driver. If there were no improvement, the ride would be Jan's.

Opperman's hopes were again dashed. It was now too late to make the Ohio Sprint Car race and it appeared too late to make Indy as well. Suddenly a breathless Routh came charging into the garage and proclaimed, "Jan, it's yours — let's get going." Together, they rushed toward the pit apron to begin one of the greatest last-ditch adventures in Indianapolis history.

"When I got out to the car, Routh's people said that they had tried everything and that I could set it up any particular way I wanted. I knew very little about those machines and here these guys were turnin' the whole thing over to me. Man, I sure wasn't any chassis expert, but I started tryin' to figure things out.

"Champ Cars ride on coil springs and shock absorber bump rubbers. I measured the tilt on the car and sure enough the left bump rubbers were hittin' before the right ones. Maybe some "Champers" run that way on the left side, but to me it was just backwards. In the Sprint Cars we tilted the other way and Sprinters were all that I really understood. So I stiffened the right side of Routh's car, put on some new tires and went out to try it out. At first the thing pushed badly, but as the tires scuffed up a bit . . . the handling started to improve. Anyway, I pulled back in, made a few final adjustments and waited for a chance to qualify."

As Jan Opperman sat waiting anxiously in the cockpit — hoping his Sprint Car mechanical know-how would stand him in good stead — the last minutes of the '76 Indy qualifying ticked off on the clock. He was next in line but Bill Engelhart — in Dick Simon's Eagle — had the track with only seconds left. Since Engelhart's speed was obviously too slow, Simon called in his driver. The signal gun was about to be fired as Opperman's crew pushed him off. By Indianapolis rules, if a car is moving down pit lane before the gun sounds, a qualification attempt will be allowed. Could he do it . . . could he make the field amidst such mind-bogling pressure? The time Jan had to beat was Eldon Rasmussen's four lap average of 180.650.

"Seated in that car, my nomex underwear soaking up the sweat, things were pretty tense," Opperman recalls. "Just as Engelhart was getting set to pull off the track, Chris Economaki stuck an ABC Television microphone in my face and started talking about there not being enough time left for me to qualify.

" 'There are only seconds left' he said, 'you're not going to make it. How does it feel to have come so close and not get the chance?'

"I replied that it wasn't up to him or me whether I made it or not — that was God's decision. It was up to God. Boy, I sure didn't need any negative thoughts laid on me at that time.

"Even after the engine was started and I was moving along pit row, I almost blew the whole deal right down the tube. Some friends of mine were standing along the fence waving and cheering. Wanting to appear cool, I raised my hand to wave back. In doing so, I accidentally hit the kill-button and killed the motor. Praise God . . . somehow I flipped the thing back on and the motor started running again. Whewie . . . cool Jan Opperman . . . no more cool for me. It's both hands on the wheel from now on."

After Opperman's engine had been allowed to warm, he was green flagged away and track announcer Tom Carnegie's electrifying voice told the story.

"He is fast enough . . . FORTY-NINE and SIXTY-SIX ONE HUNDREDTHS . . . the speed is ONE EIGHTY-ONE POINT TWO THREE TWO!!!!"

Jan's three remaining laps were even faster . . . 181.855, 181.811 and 181.965. In one of auto racing's all-time dramatic moments, Jan Opperman had thrust himself into the 1976 Indianapolis 500.

The race, itself, was slightly anticlimactic. Torrential rains permanently halted all activities after 102 laps (two circuits over the half way point). Opperman, starting dead last (thirty-third) had methodically worked his way to sixteenth position. Sixteenth was his official finishing spot. It would have been higher but for a mistake by a youthful and over-zealous crew member. On Jan's first fuel stop, the young man started over the wall to assist, catching himself too late. His temporary presence upon the scene increased the actual working force from five to six . . . a rule violation. Only five men are allowed over the wall, working on a car, at one time. For this, Jan was penalized one lap, which affected his final placement in the field.

"The Indy and Champ Car experience is a great thing for any race driver," Opperman states in retrospect. "This may sound like bragging but the whole trip was easier than I expected . . . even Indianapolis.

"Only one time did I feel real apprehensive or up-tight. That was the first time I saw Michigan International Speedway. Those high banks looked like killers to me and I couldn't imagine driving Mergard's car around that place. So I went to the one man who gives the straightest answers and tells things best the way they are . . . Bill Vukovich. He is a good driver, who is totally honest. Vukovich said Michigan's looks were deceiving . . . that it was a piece of cake. He was right; it's fast but easy to drive.

"I sincerely hope to be able to return to the Champ Cars in the future. I would love to get a shot at the newer, more slippery cars that incorporate the latest aerodynamic principles. The rides I had were all older machines — ones that were wider than the later designs. Sometimes at big tracks, like Indy or Ontario, those old animals were going slower at the end of the straightaways than at the beginning.

The wind-drag was simply grinding the speed down . . . there was nothing that I, as a driver, could do about it.

"The future . . . it's like I told Chris Economaki back in '76. God will take care of that."

> Good speed to your youthful valor, boy.
> So shall you scale the stars.
>
> Virgil

Comeback

On a muggy, summer evening in 1973 — a Williams Grove main event having just ended — Jan Opperman sat in the infield granting an interview. Lightning flashed in the distance and Opperman — the upper half of his uniform undone and tied around his waist by its sleeves — mopped at the flooding perspiration with a faded red bandana.

"Jan, how long can you keep going with this crazy stuff?" queried the interviewer.

"I hope to continue racing another ten years . . . that is unless one of these cars tears my head off," came the reply.

For the thing which I greatly feared is come upon me, and that which I was afraid of is come unto me.

Job III, 25

Three years later, at the '76 Hoosier Hundred, "Opp's" worst fears were nearly realized. His head wasn't exactly torn off but its contents received a severe scrambling. Before that ill-fated day, Jan's life had become a Levi-clad, downhill blast to fame and fortune. Since then, the path's direction has changed . . . straight up — "steeper than the steepest mountain". But Jan can still smile — he only winces slightly at his predicament. Perhaps it is because the man, displaying the large cross silk-screened on his T-shirt, has previously known the rigorous hassle of an uphill road. Today's struggle is a little different — the name has changed. Neither dope nor the dreary disillusionment of "The Sixties" will do . . . this time around we'll call it COMEBACK.

"Lots of guys have made big comebacks in auto racing," Opperman acknowledges. "Hurtubise, Kenyon, Rutherford and Lee Kunzman (who had an injury similar to mine) made it back. My mistake was tryin' to return too soon," he concedes. "Mary Lou tried to convince me that I wasn't ready — being a hard-headed 'kraut', I didn't listen. Went down to the '77 USAC Sprint opener at Salem (Indiana) and made a fool of myself. Worse than that, my reputation was damaged . . . I'm still payin' for that today.

"However, I've learned the truth and faced it. Comebacks from a thumping like I got take time. It's gonna take time for me . . . I know that now. Praise God for showin' me the light."

Jan is entirely correct in the appraisal of his reputation difficulties. It is nothing personal but rather relates to the physical damage he received in the accident. From past experience, racing people — especially car owners — are leery of drivers fighting the effects of head injuries. Chiefly because such impairments travel in the company of rather sinister bedfellows . . . things like reflex slowdowns, mental lapses and visual difficulties. Plainly, drivers who have been thoroughly whacked on the head aren't supposed to be easily reconstructed to previous ability levels.

"Yup, all those things — bad reflexes and the like — plagued me at first," Jan recollects. "I even had trouble coordinatin' activities like walkin' and blowin' my nose . . . ha, ha. Not any longer . . . if anything I am, at least, as good as before. I run three miles a day, do plenty of exercises and even my driving is better in some ways.

"My greatest problem is a lack of on-the-track aggressiveness. Sometimes my foot is a little conservative and I seem reluctant to get into close quarters," he says, shaking his head. "It's not fear — believe me . . . just a lack of confidence. Not enough competition laps, a year away from racing, and some weak rides are partly responsible for my hesitancy.

Memories of the accident don't bother me, 'cause I can't remember any of that mess."

As for the Opperman comeback, there have been numerous positive signs. A strong showing in the Ernie Dicroce Sprinter at Atlanta's decrepit Lakewood Park (Oct. '77), a victory in a spring ('78) Supermodified race at Tulsa, Oklahoma and another smashing triumph on Calistoga, California's clay (July, '78) provide the highlights so far.

Unfortunately, with the dust from his Calistoga win still hanging in the air, Jan was involved in another horrible crash. The following weekend (July 9, '78) while running the Altamont (California) pavement, Opperman's Carville-Alves Sprinter contacted another speeding vehicle and leaped into a ferocious series of end over end flips. A pursuing car — trying to avoid the melee — slid into the pits, injuring several mechanics and car owners. The publicity generated by this debacle hardly benefited Jan's cause.

"Not remembering the Hoosier Hundred crash, I'd have to say the Altamont deal was the worst I've been through," Opperman explains. "They say I went twelve times end for end . . . the ambulance even caught fire when I was being driven to the hospital. The pit area people gettin' busted up was a terrible thing. It always makes me sick when anyone gets hurt.

"In spite of the opinions of some, I can't accept all the blame for the accident . . . things like that happen during a hard-fought Sprint Car race. Here's my side of what took place. Regardless of having some difficulties with our motor, we were doin' pretty well and even won our heat. In the feature we were down one cylinder but still competitive. On the fourth lap, I lost another cylinder and slowed drastically. Some poor guy behind me had no warning and tapped my tail. That shoved me over a car in front, starting the whole thing. Thank God — because it might have been worse. Actually, some of us were very lucky that we weren't killed."

And so it has gone for Jan along the comeback highway. Some victories, some defeats and the inevitable crashes have all visited his effort. Throughout the experience — including the physical pain, financial hardship and personal frustrations — he remains steadfast in his belief that Jan Opperman is a very lucky man.

"I'm not necessarily talking about being spared in the Hoosier Hundred accident," Opperman elaborates. "No, I'm talking about my friends plus many other folks, that I didn't even know, who stepped in and gave my family a hand. When I was so broke and about to lose our home in Montana, people mailed me money from all over the United States. It was incredible. Another time, just before Christmas, a bunch of fellow racers helped me out so the kids could have a super holiday.

"Then there were other long-time pals like Ernie Dicroce and "Doc" Miller. Both of these guys own Sprint Cars. Ernie is an ol' Italiano from Denver, with a heart of gold. He was goin' through some rough financial times himself and yet he dragged his car all over the country for me to drive. "Doc" was just as good to me. He is a chiropractor down in Tampa, who drives his own Sprinter. "Doc" really wanted to compete in the 1980 Florida Nationals . . . it was a great dream of his. But when I was having trouble landing a ride for the same meet, he turned his car and mechanic over to me. It takes real men of God to do unselfish things like that.

"Considering these examples of friendship and human kindness, does anyone believe I'm not a lucky man?"

There is one other subject — related to the Opperman comeback — which causes Jan great concern. It has to do with quitting . . . a word which tends to irritate Jan.

"People keep asking (some even suggest) why I don't quit . . . retire from racing," he notes with a frown. That sort of talk gets to me. First of all, auto racing is and has been my profession . . . it's the way I've put food on the table. Until I am positive that it is impossible to return, I refuse to quit. Nobody wants to give up a career, unless it is absolutely necessary. Race drivers are no different than other people . . . they cling to what they know best.

"But there is more to not quitting than that. Everyone has a hero . . . well, Jesus is my hero and Jesus was never a quitter. He could have come down off that cross if he'd chosen to do so. No way . . . not Jesus . . . he stuck to his guns even as they drove the nails into him. He wouldn't forsake his beliefs or his faith. I'm not comparing myself to Jesus Christ . . . understand that. Still a man looks to his heroes for help in troubled times. When the moment comes to pack up the racing, I'll know about it. God — my Boss — will tell me. Right now I believe he intends for me to continue trying. The Lord has faith in it and so do I."

As this book draws to a close, I find Jan's thoughts on quitting to be not at all surprising. The entire volume deals with a man who has seemed incapable of comprehending the definition of such a word as quit. In fact, the essence of his message is aimed in the opposite direction . . . KEEP ON GOING . . . though it may hurt. And that he has . . . whether it be in the final qualifying seconds at Indianapolis or during the cruel aftermath of his brother's death . . . through it all Jan Opperman has kept on going.

Will his comeback be successful? As Jan would say . . . "only God knows". But don't bet against its success, because dreams die hard beneath the broad brim of a weathered Western hat.

If the triumphant return is impossible, then shed no tears for "Oppie". He will still be better off than most of us. JESUS is his hero and Jan Opperman is thoroughly dialed-in with THE LORD.

The Lord is my light and my salvation; whom shall I fear? The Lord is the strength of my life, of whom shall I be afraid?

Psalms 24:7

JAN OPPERMAN'S INDIANAPOLIS CAR RECORD

Event	Finish	Starting Position	Car Name	Laps	Reason	Date
			1974			
Indianapolis 500	21	32	Viceroy Special	85	Blew tire	5/26/74
Pocono 500	33	14	Viceroy Special	4	Overheating motor	6/30/74
			1976			
Indianapolis 500	16	33	Routh Meat Packing	97	Rain	5/30/76
Pocono 500	19	32	Mergard Racing	145	Running at finish	6/27/76
Michigan Int. Spdy.	7	16	Mergard Racing	97	Running at finish	7/18/76
Trenton Spdy.	10	14	Longhorn Racing	113	Running at finish	8/15/76
Ontario, Calif. 500	6	23	Longhorn Racing	194	Running at finish	9/ 5/76

MAJOR TRACK RECORDS HELD BY JAN OPPERMAN AT TIME OF HIS 1976 ACCIDENT

UNITED STATES AUTO CLUB (Sprint Cars)

Track	Distance	Record	Date	Car
Indiana State Fairgrounds (1 mile dirt)	1 lap	106.765 MPH	7/31/76	Longhorn Racing Special
Erie County Fairgrounds/ Hamburg, NY (1/2 mile dirt)	8 laps	72.913 MPH	8/27/76	Longhorn Racing Special
Reading Fairgrounds (1/2 mile dirt)	1 lap	78.982 MPH	7/ 3/74	Speedway Motors
Williams Grove Spdy. (1/2 mile dirt)	8 laps	74.451 MPH	9/22/73	Bali-Hi Motor Hotel Special

IMCA

Track	Distance	Record	Date	Car
Tampa Fairgrounds	6 laps	2:38.37	2/10/74	Speedway Motors
(1/2 mile dirt)	8 laps	3:31.17	2/10/74	Speedway Motors

OUTLAWS

Track	Distance	Record	Date	Car
Williams Grove Spdy.	10 laps	3:47.90	8/ 3/73	Bogar Special
Belleville, Kansas (1/2 mile dirt)	1 lap	19.06	8/29/75	Speedway Motors

A PARTIAL LISTING OF JAN OPPERMAN'S ACCOMPLISHMENTS IN DIRT RACING

1971 — Knoxville Sprint Car Nationals Champion (Knoxville, Iowa)

1971 — Western States Sprint Champion (Phoenix, Arizona)

1972 — Western States Sprint Champion (Phoenix, Arizona)

1972 — An amazing year for Opperman. 100 dirt races were started producing 44 feature wins and 12 second place finishes. Possibly this is the greatest season ever put together by a dirt driver.

1973 — Selinsgrove Speedway Champion (Selinsgrove, Pa.)

1974 — IMCA Winternational Sprint Champion (Tampa, Fla.)

1975 — IMCA Winternational Sprint Champion (Tampa, Fla.)

1975 — Big Car Racing Association Champion

1975 — Northwest Dirt Cup Series Champion

1976 — Hullman Classic Winner, Terre Haute (USAC)

1979 — Named Sprint Car Driver of the Decade by Stock Car Racing Magazine

I am an Outlaw. I was born an Outlaw's son.
The Highway is my Legacy, on the Highway I will Run.
In one hand I've a Bible, in the other I got a Gun.
Don't you know me?
I'm the Man who won.
Woman don't try to love me, don't try to understand.
A life upon the road is the life of an Outlaw . . . Man.

Lines from "The Eagles"
recording "Outlaw Man",
included in their Desperado
Album by Asylum Records.

The Bogar Special - looking its very best at Tampa in 1973. (Tom Dick)

Hooked up with the Terre Haute clay in the Longhorn . . .August, 1976. (Mahoney)

Jan Opperman ~ February 9th 1939 to September 4th 1997

POSTSCRIPT

JULY 6, 1981

Just as this book began with a devastating racing crash — so, apparently, is it destined to end with one.

While driving a URC Sprint car race at Jennerstown (Pa.) Speedway, June 20, "Oppie" took the heavy hit, once again. It occurred on a restart — those ever-deadly restarts. He was movin' full-tilt — smokin' the boys on the outside — when he contacted a competitor's car. One of the regular deals for a rim-rider.

Up and over — a flip, maybe more, and Jan's Stanton blasted a concrete wall, bottom first. Car owner Claude Stanley theorizes that Opperman's injuries came about as follows.

> "The car hit the wall with terrible force. The lower-left frame rail was pushed in about eight inches or more. That's where the belts attach and it let Jan flop around pretty bad as they loosened up. He must have hit his head on something, after that.
>
> "Priase God, for Gary Stanton's good car. A lesser one would have come apart completely in such a bad crash. The cage wasn't even damaged. Jan is hurt bad — still, it could've been worse."

Hurt badly, for sure — it was the head trip returning for an encore performance. Jan Opperman — on his back and unconscious. He was in Pittsburgh's Presbyterian Hospital — the Intensive Care Section; condition listed as critical and in a coma.

"Oppie" shouldered a heavy load this time — maybe worse than before. Violent neuromuscular convulsions shook his body. His reflexes were running wild. Next, and typical of head injuries, he went the opposite direction. Total rigidity — no muscular action at all.

The brain was swelling, there was a contusion on its left side. Neurosurgeons drilled the skull and inserted a tube to drain liquid. The swelling had to be contained — pressure against the skull could result in permanent brain damage.

Meanwhile, Jan's lungs were filling with fluid. His reflexes not working, Opperman couldn't cough up the collecting liquid. Tubes were run down both his throat and nose — the fluid had to be kept out. If not, he would contact pneumonia and surely die.

Plainly, for the second time in five years, "Opp" was locked in a life and death struggle.

By the following Wednesday (June 24) the rigidity began to disappear. His neuromuscular system was starting to relax. Only his left arm and hand were still rigid. Eventually, they, too, relaxed.

This is not to be confused with paralysis. Electroencephalograms indicated proper brain reactions. Hence, there was no true paralysis. Continual scanning caused doctors to be hopeful for recovery. The brain was functioning normally.

The coma continued. The decision was made to do a tracheotomy. Thus, breathing difficulty would be eased. Much of his face swelling diminished following this procedure.

❧

Wednesday, July 1 — good news greeted everyone. Brain swelling was under control and the drain could be removed. Almost immediately Jan began showing signs of waking up. His eyes opened — there was body movement. Gradually, he seemed to recognize Mary, his Mom and others. His lips tried to form words — he squeezed hands. But "Oppie" still slept most of the time. Partly because of heavy sedation, necessary for the continuing brain exams. And, like it or not, the coma's influence had not been entirely overcome.

Fourth of July weekend — more good news. Jan was removed from the Neurosurgical Intensive Care Section and placed in a more normal hospital situation. I was told by an Intensive Care nurse that the entire department was pleased with "Opp's" progress.

So there you have it — that's where we are now. At the very best — from the most optimistic angle, Jan Opperman is in for a long recovery period.

Will he ever race again? Most likely not. His age is against it. His wife says no. His mother says no. Even Jan's young son told grandma by phone — "Daddy has gotta find a new way to feed us. We can't let him get hurt again."

That pretty well says it all. We can't let him get hurt again. Ironically, for the first time since the original accident, "Opp" appeared to be getting his racing program together. There were flashes of hope.

Sadly, life is frequently unfair — even to the fairest of men.

"Lord Jesus Christ, easy my sufferings and make me well again. Grant me full health so that I may be restored to your service."
Chaplain's Prayer

Printed in the United States
94703LV00001B/35/A